KEELS ON WHEELS

H.A. DOUGLAS

Illustrations by Rob Moehr

DEDICATION

To boat owners, whose behaviour is often funny, sometimes bizarre always fascinating. You have enabled me to eke out a living and provide the stories for this book. Some who have not been included may wish they had been and some may regret their inclusion. Some names have been changed to 'protect the innocent' as they say. Some have been left unchanged to implicate the guilty!

To the many drivers who passed our way before we discovered boat transport, the relationship was for mutual benefit and your contributions were greatly appreciated.

To Neil, or Admiral'Q' or just 'Q' who started with us in 1987 with the strongest work ethic of anyone I have ever known and whose contribution to the business has been immeasurable.

To Mum, who liked the written word and in a different time would have had her writing published.

To Paul and Iain, sons to be proud of and great dads too. Different in many ways but with common standards and values.

To my wife Angela, for over fifty years of patience, love and affection. Still my best friend.

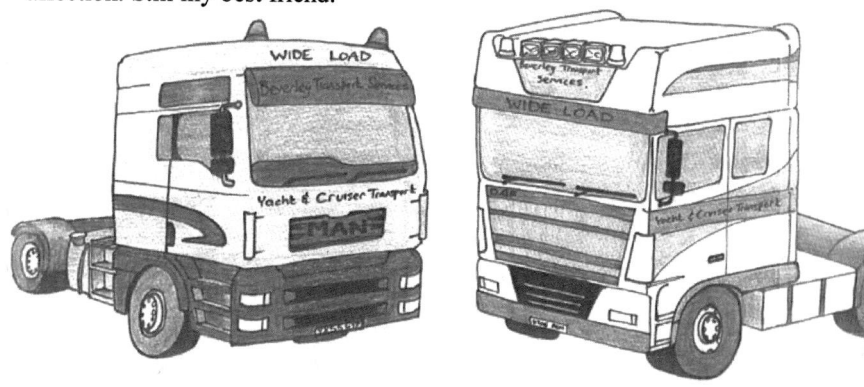

Big Mandy, Dafney, Little Mandy and Dobbin

KEELS ON WHEELS

The Adventures of Dobbin, Dafney, Little Mandy, Big Mandy & Friends

Copyright © 2013 H. A. Douglas

First published in Great Britain in 2013 by Riverhead

All rights reserved.
No part of this publication may be reproduced, stored in a retrieval system, or transmitted, in any form or by any means, without the prior written permission of the publisher, nor be otherwise circulated in any form of binding or cover other than that in which it is published and without a similar condition being imposed on the subsequent publisher.

H. A. Douglas has asserted his right to be identified as the author of this work under the Copyright, Designs and Patents Act 1988.

A CIP catalogue record for this book is available from the British Library

ISBN 978-0-9567782-7-7

Design and Production by Riverhead, Hull
44-46 High Street, Hull, East Yorkshire. HU1 1PS
Telephone: 01482 318218
email: mike@riverheadbooks.karoo.co.uk

Printed by: Fisk Printers, Hull

CONTENTS

'Are You Busy Dad?'	7
Bit Of A Jolly	15
Dobbin Gives In	26
Tipped & Brassed Up	31
Mad Max Comes Home	38
Time To Get Serious	45
You Can't Do Enough For A Good Boss	53
Boats & Boaters	75
Gardens, Fields & Driveways	101
Knock, Knock, Knockin' On Dobbin's Door	111
A Bad Dose Of Eczema	124
Scotland's Wasted On You	139
Classics & 'Wafis'	152
Tupperware Boxes & Gin Palaces	172
Fishing Boats & Workboats	196
Police & Pretend Police	214
Marinas & Boatyards	220
Any Way The Wind Blows	231

CHAPTER ONE

'Are You Busy Dad?'

There is nothing more gratifying than the love and affection shown by a child to a parent. Our son Paul is a good example of this and as a teenager would telephone every day from work to enquire after his Mum's well-being. The conversation would perhaps run on these lines;

"What's for tea? I'll be in at six and out straight away, so I need it ready!"

"Where are you going?" his mum might ask, in response to his concerned enquiry.

"Out."

"Where to?"

"Just Out!"

"Who with?"

"With me mates."

Thus ended the 'care and concern' conversation between Mother and Son.

So, as well as manning the 'phone, looking after much of the paperwork for the business, maintaining the domestic scene with cooking, washing, ironing, dusting and hoovering and running Paul's younger brother, Iain, to and from school, Angela was also required to have Paul's meal on the table when he came home!

'Gracious, long suffering, tolerant and accommodating,' would perhaps be appropriate terms for Angela who has put up with the nonsense of road transport with acceptance and stoicism. She's a lovely lady and has always set very high standards for herself, and thankfully both Paul and Iain in different ways have inherited these qualities. It will soon become apparent to the reader that no such attributes can be ascribed to the writer.

But back to the fateful mealtime, set in the late 1980s when Fords still had rear wheel drive and the best music was Dire Straits. For Paul, preparation for the evening could be summarised as the 'Three S's', which included a shave and a shower. He might perhaps have time, subject to a pause in the incessant phone calls that plague the business, to have a brief conversation with me.

Looking back, we have lived a life dominated by the telephone. Paul will tell you that when he was in trouble, the international statement from mothers everywhere, "You just wait 'til your father gets home," cut no ice in our household.

He says, "I couldn't even get a bollocking for the blooming phone ringing!" as he had to wait for a lull in conversations in order to get a telling off.

Iain also, on another occasion, laid with concussion near the nurses' station in Hull Royal Infirmary after being knocked off his bike, hearing the ward phone ringing continuously, muttered, "Just like home" and drifted off to sleep.

This oppression by telephone is one reason why we have a genuine red telephone box in the garden. The area where we live never had red telephone boxes. They were white and operated by Hull City Council. Come the privatisation of state and municipal assets, this enterprise was 'shared out' providing the Council and many private individuals with generous windfalls. Another justification for the phone box is that Angela likes, or at least used to like, cleaning windows and a 'phone box has seventy-five panes of glass, which means one hundred and fifty sides and six hundred corners if you really like window cleaning! Paul gave her the handle "Window Woman" when CB radios were all the rage.

"Are you busy Dad?" Paul enquired during his brief

Busy, just busy

encounter with domestic facilities. His question referred to the state of the business, not my personal exertions. Oh yes, we are busy all right, it's always *busy* in road transport!

You could be '*Busy*' looking for work to keep the wheels turning, '*Busy*' making bookings that you and your drivers will keep but the customer probably will not, so you'll be '*busy*' re-booking jobs at the last minute.

'*Busy*' could be squeezing an extra job in to try to turn a bad week into a reasonable one.

'*Busy*' could be arriving at a supermarket distribution centre and being told, "You are not booked in, get back in your cab and wait!"

'*Busy*' could be frantically trying to sort out faulty paperwork when a load is rejected or begging to be unloaded to be able to get to your next delivery on time.

'*Busy*' could be trying to get paid for work done weeks or even months ago or grovelling to the bank manager for an extension of the overdraft.

'*Busy*' could be trying to get a tyre replaced on a motorway on a Friday afternoon.

No, a 'busy' haulage business is not necessarily profitable. It's probably an organisation desperately trying to earn a living for its owners and employees. There is a very valid saying, "In transport it's easy to spend a pound and earn sixty pence"

"A bit patchy!" was my reply to Paul, a reflection of the vagaries of work levels.

"What about Dobbin?" he asked.

That's a strange question, I thought.

Paul worked at a truck rental company and thus had exposure to the workings of the haulage industry, an industry based on idealism, optimism, foolhardiness, vivid imagination and considerable abuse. He would come home with tales about other operators; some good ones, some cowboys and many in between struggling along much like us. Paul would often see an opportunity to pass on to me in the hope of improving the status, profile and profitability of this business. Not academic but gifted with astute reasoning and common sense, Paul asserted that he *went* to school but gained nothing from it. He was allergic to pen and paper, an affliction which continued into adult life, but overcame this handicap with good manners and thorough communications' skills. He was happy to pay Iain to write his 'Thank You' letters at Christmas and birthdays, a subterfuge of mutual benefit as Iain was more than willing to accept payment for this task.

Paul was, and is, tidy, smart and thoroughly professional in all his chosen activities, inheriting high standards from his Mum. He tried removing the dirty linen basket when he left home, believing it might work in his own house.

"Well you throw the dirty stuff into the magic basket and it re-appears on the shelf, washed, ironed and refreshed!"

He also declared that when he left we would become impoverished due to the withdrawal of his housekeeping payments or 'Board'. Some chance!

However, to enquire about Dobbin took me by surprise as it was the last vehicle for Paul to have shown concern for. At the time, we owned, well, to be honest we didn't own, but we had loans for, and operated, three fairly new vehicles; a Volvo, an ERF and a Mercedes, plus a very old Scania. We hired extra units when required, pulling refrigerated trailers for various food producers. Dobbin was also a Mercedes, but somewhat long in the tooth. 'He' was the scourge of some of the drivers, being very basic, visually somewhat plain and rather slow!

Originally bought as a 'shunter' to serve the main motors by bringing loaded trailers from customers' premises to the yard and returning empty ones, this Merc' received little TLC from Paul or indeed from anyone else. Promoted due to a crisis in the business, one of many, Dobbin had once again to 'go down the road' a situation causing much grumbling among the drivers. Given that HGV drivers are a breed who can grumble and whinge about just about anything, having this old truck inflicted upon them brought about derisive comments on an epic scale. Registered on a 'W' plate from the first time round, this Merc lacked driver appeal and was somewhat old. From a driver's point of view it was no "home from home" but it still had some life left in it and was equipped with two bunks. When a driver complained about having to drive the Merc, I would berate him with a fervent defence and reasons to tolerate Dobbin's limitations and sensibilities.

"Listen! Dobbin always starts, steers, stops, and is warm, comfortable and utterly reliable. If he takes an hour longer to do a job it's an hour more pay for you. He's paid for and if you look after him, he will be there for you or someone else to drive tomorrow!"

Truck cleaning classes

    These attributes had led to the truck being christened the somewhat dubious but entirely appropriate nickname, derived from a faithful, plodding donkey from the early days of black and white TV. Paul spent much of his spare time cleaning and polishing our trucks and trailers, making them a well-respected, 'tidy fleet'. Even when still at school he would rush home to change, deny that he had any homework or claim to have done it at school, disappear to the yard and keep the vehicles in a pristine condition. This support from a teenager was particularly welcome and he would always decline our offers to help. Despite the heavy burden of cleaning up to five units and trailers, Paul even found time to run training courses for potential cleaners. Surprisingly, or perhaps not, the recruits for these courses were all girls. If we called at the yard during the evening we often found him training young 'laydees' in the skills of washing, cleaning and polishing. Sometimes we also found the curtains drawn in one of the cabs as Paul demonstrated the arrangement of the bunks

***Dobbin, neglected in the corner**†*

and other facilities.

We eventually discovered that from the age of around fourteen, Paul had 'borrowed' the company van to "impress the chicks" and reduce his need for driving lessons when the legal age was attained. In later years Paul's car and his own truck would receive the same loving care and attention and would always look immaculate. Dobbin, unfortunately, would not respond to Paul's efforts and remained clean but rather drab.

"So, why this sudden interest in Dobbin?" I enquired.

"This bloke wants us to hire him an artic unit to pull a trailer for moving boats. He has no Operator's License, nor HGV license so we can't help him. I reckon it would just suit Dobbin, plodding along with a boat on his back! Will you meet Captain Maxwell Griffin (hereafter called 'Mad Max') and stop him pestering us?" replied Paul.

How prophetic was Paul's judgement. And so began our foray into the boating world and the practice of moving

"Keels on Wheels"!

Obviously, to develop a boat transport division would be a logical extension of refrigerated distribution.

In a business employing up to twenty men, who cares if the boss is absent, riding around the nicer parts of the British Isles for days at a time? The necessary investment in specialised equipment and procedures would be carefully calculated, assessed and resources committed. Each aspect of this new and potentially profitable activity would be carefully scrutinised and deliberated upon before any decisions were made. Market Research, Cash Flow predictions and Customer Profiling would naturally be thoroughly investigated.

In short, this opportunity required the preparation of a detailed Business Plan, a roadmap for business success, a formal statement of a set of goals and the means to achieve them.

So, I said, *"Ooh that sounds interesting, let's have a go!"*

CHAPTER TWO
Bit Of A Jolly

It seemed entirely appropriate to meet Mr. Griffin on board a boat. It would give me some idea what this new project would entail, so one cold, wet January evening I ventured to the edge of one of the old docks which had become Hull Marina. Surrounded by security fencing and requiring a swipe device to open a gate, I paced up and down trying to catch someone's attention to let me in. It seemed that people on boats are not usually identified by their name. I asked one or two people if they knew Mr. Griffin but all I got in response was; "What's he on?" Did they mean medication or perhaps drugs? No, they wanted to know the name of the boat he came from!

Eventually, a voice boomed across the water and I was ordered to wait for entry.

"Mad Max", the character but for whom, none of the following adventures would have happened, resembled a grumpy version of Popeye the Sailor. He was tall, with thinning hair and a straggly ginger beard. A sea dog from head to foot, with an irascible, temperamental disposition who appeared somewhat intimidating in manner.

"I don't exist" he barked, as he led me along the walkways of the marina, floating structures called pontoons or sometimes 'fingers'. Boats of various types - sailing yachts and motor cruisers in particular - were attached, or moored, to these pontoons and I marvelled at the opulence and affluence that these vessels represented, I was surely to enter a craft of luxury and style.

Max climbed over a stretch of trip-wire that ran

Cramped Cabin Conference

round the deck of a yacht and I followed him down the dimly lit, almost vertical stairs to the cabin, or 'down below'. In the gloom Max shuffled along a sort of seat, squeezing against a small table with a big tube or pole holding it to the floor and to the roof of the cabin. I wondered what stresses and strains would make it necessary to hold a table up with such a massive support. I squeezed along the other side of the table and prepared to make notes and discuss Max's proposals.

"I don't pay tax and I don't claim benefits, I just live on peoples' boats, do a few jobs on them and move them around" asserted my host, justifying his situation. His murky surroundings comprised a small cooking range, a few small round windows, a door to a toilet and another to a sleeping compartment. Not much luxury here for sure. But I was to learn that proper sailors love these conditions. When they have endured hours of cold wet exposure on the deck, hanging over the side to try to stabilise the boat, skimming the waves with their backsides, winding the sails up and down to gain speed or wind resistance, they can shelter in wet, cramped spaces down below. They just love the discomfort because it is heaven sent; all the wind, rain, snow, spray and sleet is free, and so is the claustrophobia of the cabin.

Max's current project was to take some fin keeled yachts from Hull Marina to Gairloch in North West Scotland.

Definition: a fin keel is one where a flat board, solid and heavy, extends out of the bottom of the boat. This is to counter the activities of the sailors trying to turn the boat on its' side when sailing 'close to the wind' or somesuch nautical term.

The boats were owned by one of his "customers" who had chartered them out for a season to a business in Badachro, a small community on the southern shore of Loch Gairloch. This business had cottages and Day Boats for hire and would add these Moody 32s to their portfolio. Max's client had a trailer, a low loader with a single axle on steel springs, with adjustable supports to 'cradle' the boat and had a deep recess to get the boat keel low down. Although it was fairly old, it was 'in test'.

A motto of this business, when a new opportunity is offered, was always, "Say Yes, and then wriggle." This represents a certain amount of foolhardiness and often leads to embarrassment or worse. On this occasion, ignorance of the techniques for loading and moving boats was over-ruled by the anticipation and excitement of doing something new, something a bit different and the thought of going to Scotland. Maybe this love of Scotland is hereditary. My parents loved the country and took many holidays there. Our ancestors were apparently members of gypsy groups roaming the hills of Galloway. For whatever reason, being able to travel to Scotland whilst working had a certain strong attraction to me and still tends to distort my thinking! Mad Max outlined the terms and rates that

Spinal Recovery

established boat hauliers would be likely to charge and we agreed prices for the project. Max would be a passenger for the first trip as he was going to stay in Badachro to help with the charter business.

Our negotiations concluded, I climbed up to the deck of the yacht and came ashore. Within a couple of hours I could walk upright again.

My delight at the prospect of trips to Scotland generated some concern amongst my family and staff. Considering the fragility of the business and the dreadful financial situation, the boss's absence carrying people's 'toys' to the far end of the country in the middle of winter did not seem sensible.

"A bit of a Jolly," perhaps and why not I thought, relishing the prospect of the wonderful mountains, lochs and glens. Come to think of it, it is a sad fact that the one individual whose absence is not missed, is that of the boss.

Trusted drivers were charged with keeping the show on the road while I was away. The cellphone system was in its infancy but might work in the less remote areas we would be crossing, so some contact would be possible, perhaps. My work would, after all, be pioneering, forging a new dimension to our business. I would be driving, or perhaps the word should be, sailing into uncharted waters!

"This could be the start of new and profitable activities," I confidently predicted, but not really believing that this could be anything more than an occasional ride out. This sort of work couldn't be regular, could it?

It turned out that Dobbin was not quite ready for the job. He wouldn't fit under Mad Max's trailer. Modifications were carried out at Paul's place of work enabling, if you'll excuse the expression, proper coupling to take place! But then Dobbin developed another frustrating trait. He revved freely in neutral in the workshop but on the road was out of breath even with an empty trailer. As the time for our 'maiden voyage' approached there was no time to sort him out, despite considerable attention from the specialists. He would have to go, breathless if necessary.

Under Mad Max's bombastic supervision, the first yacht was loaded at Hull Marina and Dobbin was prepared for the long journey. Max imparted the number one golden rule for loading boats; get the keel as low as possible taking the weight, then tighten up the flexible supports to stop the boat falling over! These supports effectively become a cradle. He also introduced me to some other critical concepts such as measuring the travelling height and knowing the width of the craft. The load has then to be strapped down with the points of contact insulated with bits of carpet or other padding to prevent chafing and the police have to be informed if the load exceeds a certain width.

Our subsequent competence can be ascribed to Mad Max's early tuition, freely and vociferously given. Dobbin's performance gave cause for concern. There was considerable pursing of lips and stroking of chins, with authoritative voices delivering diverse opinions.

"It'll be this or that," but no cure was found. I made a big mistake in thinking that Dobbin would not notice the weight of the boat, which only added about five tons to the payload.

In one respect Dobbin was very environmentally friendly. Wildlife was safe from the approach of this lorry. Bees, flies, moths and butterflies could simply glide out of the way rather than splatter into the windscreen as there was plenty of time 'to go round'. This saved on washer fluid too. Even hedgehogs could scuttle away from Dobbin's approaching wheels.

So, one Sunday afternoon in February, around dusk, we set off complete with flasks of tea and several days' supply of cheese and Marmite sarnies.

This, the first pioneering boat trip, from Hull to Gairloch in North West Scotland, was a distance of around five-hundred miles. Unless going downhill where gravity would give assistance, about thirty-five miles an hour was about the best the asthmatic Dobbin could achieve. After a while it became painfully obvious that all projections of arrival times would be futile. And keeping to the Drivers' Hours Regulations would be impossible for a vehicle achieving little more than walking pace on some parts of the journey. There would have to be some 'creative tachography!' Road transport operates under very strict rules and regulations particularly for the hours that drivers can spend at work. Historically, these rules have been monitored firstly by log books, where the driver could write about his imaginary journey in sections such as 'hours worked', time spent driving and periods taken as 'rest'.

Would you believe, some drivers falsified the information so they could work for longer than the rules allowed! So the Ministry of Transport, then the European

Union devised tachographs, mechanical devices which recorded the vehicle's activities more accurately and then made them electronic and digital, each successive step challenging the drivers' ingenuity. Then the Working Time Directive was invoked, adding another tier of regulations which complicated matters even further and provided opportunity for more trainers, more scrutiny, more fiddling and more expense.

But of course, we didn't run 'bent', as some hauliers did, well not much anyway. Not even every day. Not excessively. Well not too excessively, just enough to get us to safe parking, or more likely, the pub. In the long term it turns out that boatyards and marinas and as a consequence boat transport, operate under a very benign regime. Schoolteachers look on enviously at the hours worked by boatyards and marinas. So nowadays we never need to challenge the rules.

However, this journey was to be of epic duration and if I recall correctly, the first shift only got us as far as Tebay on the M6. Mad Max was already showing signs of agitation. After all this time it should be safe to confess that a 'donor card' or perhaps several donor cards were used to carry out this journey. Elaboration of this procedure, which is not about donating organs upon death, could perhaps lead to prosecution so, "nuff said".

It was a long, slow, tiring yet inspiring journey. Beyond Inverness there was no cellphone coverage and it was snowing almost continuously.

At Tarvie, on the A385 there was, and hopefully still is, a sanctuary for tired drivers. A small café, set back off the road, provides food and drink both in variety and abundance either sitting down in the café or served through a hole in the wall.

This well-known and much loved caterer would be our last link with civilisation. Cards and pictures of lorries, which had called over many years formed a colourful

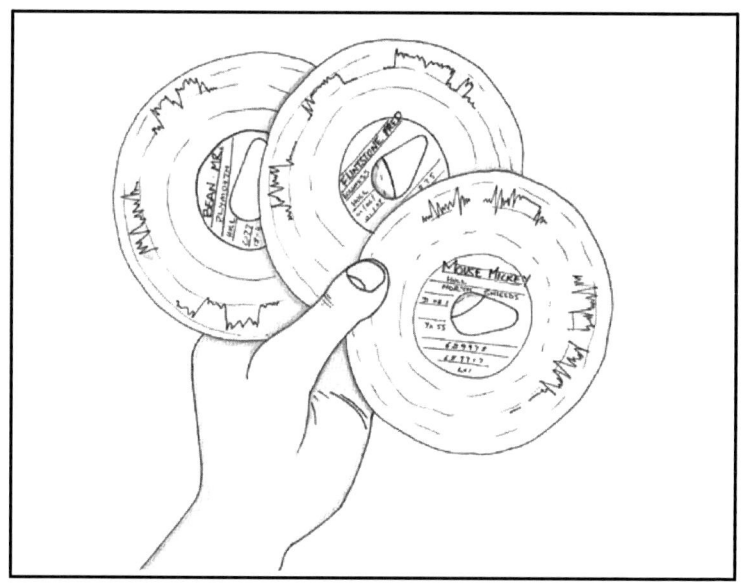

Donor Cards

gallery on the café walls. I proffered a picture of Dobbin but it showed him pulling a fridge and was probably not worthy of inclusion amongst more distinguished company. Half a dozen chaffinches, birds found in profusion in the car park, alighted on Dobbin's mirrors, anointing him with guano for good luck on the journey. From here-on there would be no telephone, no garages, no cafes and little else but the bleak winter landscape. The mountains of Wester Ross, spectacular and colourful in summer sunshine, become intimidating and daunting in the bleak moods of winter. At Braemore, the main road heads north towards Ullapool, while we turned onto the A382 and headed south west towards Gairloch. The road climbs in several stages to reach over a thousand feet and then drops again to sea level.

Snow was settling on the lee side of the hills and traction on the steeper slopes was becoming more and more difficult. Dobbin getting wheel spin added insult to injury. Given the minimal amount of power reaching the

Westerbus Embarrassment

wheels, traction should have been certain and positive.

"Get a grip Dobbin, get a grip!"

The last forty-five miles took nine hours! Dobbin thought he was the Ice Road Trucker going steadily and bravely where no other vehicle could go and would be one of the last vehicles to reach Gairloch that wintry night. But we were escorted much of the way by the Westerbus which contemptuously passed the struggling, sliding Dobbin several times and then diverted to deliver passengers to villages lying off the main route. Mad Max kept remarking how often we had been passed by the same bus and was grumpily sulking, probably bored by the length of time this journey was taking. We skirted Gruinard Bay, near the notorious Gruinard Island, scene of Anthrax experiments in 1942. Max remarked somewhat sarcastically, that the area was noted for the sublime influence of the Gulf Stream and as we passed Inverewe Gardens near Poolewe the roads became slightly less treacherous.

Arriving mid-evening in February there was nowhere to buy food or drink but Max's and therefore our customers held a celebration to greet their first large sailing boat. After supper and several beers, the people settled our account.

"Wow! This isn't work is it; right fair it just isn't work!"

I had recently been doing some calculations for our bank. We settled our suppliers' bills for fuel, maintenance, insurance, sundries etc. on average within twenty-four days but we were paid by our customers at an average of seventy-eight days, a disastrous disparity. And here we were paid virtually on arrival, not actually having completed the delivery! A lesson to be learned here I thought, but not learned soon enough.

The next morning a crane arrived from Inverness and the yacht was off-loaded into the crystal clear waters of Loch Gairloch. Leaving Mad Max behind as a kind of consultant cum hired hand, depending on his mood, I set off back towards Inverness. The Gulf Stream must have kicked in overnight for the journey back towards Inverness was in Spring-like sunshine. Relieved of the burden of the yacht and the one-sided conversation with Max, I travelled through the mountains with much food for thought and enough cheese and Marmite sarnies for the return journey.

Talk about being slow on the uptake! It would take another ten years for me to realise that moving boats would be enough to provide a living. I did not think there would be enough regular work to enable me to dispense with the other activities of the business. Our 'bread and butter' work was not with our own vehicles although we had several good customers providing us with work for our refrigerated trailers. Our main income was the operation of a driver agency, supplying PSV and HGV drivers to the coaching and haulage industries. We started this service in the late Seventies principally as a way of me sneaking into professional driving work. A schoolteacher is virtually unemployable in other activities and after having wearied in the job after several years in the classroom, a life on the open road seemed very appealing. Agency driving gave me the practice and experience of many types of haulage work and our customers represented a broad range of activities. Some were straightforward general hauliers' work but we also supplied tipper operators, ready-mix concrete producers, seed and plant growers, beef and poultry processors and even coffin makers. The latter activity would alone provide enough stories for a book; undertakers having a distinctive, often humorous attitude to life and of course death. The agency could have made serious money for a while but I felt that if a haulier was prepared to pay for the services of a driver, then the driver should have the bulk of that payment. On the other hand, employing drivers to hire out to other hauliers always seemed like pimping, with the best drivers always in demand but some of them behaved as though they had PMT!

The less effective drivers would always try to avoid the difficult jobs. Some could be sent anywhere and would adapt to the customers' requirements. With some it was 'horses for courses' and we employed many colourful characters. The agency provided a living; it would be some time before boat transport could fulfil that role.

Back in to Vodafone reception, the joys of boating receded as hassle from other activities occupied my thoughts. There had been no great disasters during the period of 'radio silence' but a long list of 'things to do' presented itself. Max's trailer needed a bit of attention to keep it roadworthy but it was interesting to note that being around the marina generated attention from other potential customers.

CHAPTER THREE

Dobbin Gives In

Subsequent journeys to Badachro were not without incident. We employed around twenty drivers at the time including a number of part timers. Being progressive, conscientious employers we urged all staff to join a Trade Union. In fact it was compulsory for access to docks and many industrial sites. Our promotion of the T& G W U extended to having a Shop Steward - a long haired, left wing, alcoholic, union activist named Pete Boland. Despite his politics Pete was a good worker apart from a hopeless record for bad timekeeping. His assertion that the work always got done despite his lateness helped to keep him in his job. He had, like myself, grown up in Leeds and we maintained that we were in East Yorkshire 'doing missionary work'. (After the Vikings conquered York, they divided their territory into three *Thridings,* nowadays called *Ridings).* Our apparent contempt for the East Riding was based on a number of factors, some less relevant now than in the 70s and 80s.

Firstly, the area was a cultural, social and commercial backwater at the end of the M62 Motorway or the Trans Pennine Railway according to your mode of travel. Its people were, and still are to some extent, insular and despite having a great sea-faring tradition, most Hull people rarely venture far. Indeed, East Hull residents stay in the east and those in West Hull invariably stay in the west. The 'local boy made good' had been to college in York and came back to Hull to a hero's welcome. When the Humber Bridge was completed its function seemed to be to give the more adventurous north bank inhabitants the chance to visit Barton for a pub meal on a Saturday night.

The contrast between *West* and *East* Yorkshire would also be reflected in the diversity of products and services.

For example, a DIY enthusiast buying sand at a builders' merchants in Leeds would elicit a request to be more specific such as, "Do you want sharp sand, soft sand, brown sand or yellow sand?"

In Hull, the same question would get the reply, "The sand's over there, help yourself".

In other words there was more choice in the West Riding. However, being isolated was not all to the detriment of East Yorkshire as life was less frenetic, the roads less congested and the cost of living much lower than in the West of the county.

Pete shared my love of the countryside especially Scotland. Therefore, as a dedicated and diligent employee, wishing to support the development of the boat moving side of the business, Pete joined me on a trip to Scotland. This pious motive is of course complete nonsense. Pete merely seized an opportunity to invest in his second favourite product, whisky.

After loading a bilge keel yacht in Liverpool we were flagged down by a police motorcyclist. (Note the technical term 'bilge keel'. It means two plates sticking out of the bottom of the boat, which the owner will tell you enable the boat to stand upright on its own but in most cases will impinge on the wheel arches of your trailer and complicate loading procedures). We could have been in trouble as we had failed to notify the wide load, a requirement if the width exceeds nine foot six inches and the bilge keeler measured ten.

"I don't know if youse had noticed but the tide's gone out," the policemen shouted in a thick Scouse accent, meaning the accent was thick not the copper of course. He laughed to see our anxiety at being pulled over but allowed us to proceed. Dobbin huffed and puffed as far as Inverness that night, in time for us to embark on the purpose of the trip; to promote the products of malted barley, hops and other grains! At Badachro the next evening, we offloaded the boat, they had a party and they paid us.

The next trip involved collecting an old van body from Lincolnshire, lettered up for Cadbury's if I remember correctly. This was balanced on the swan neck of the trailer, stabilised with a stack of pallets. Behind this was placed a small cruiser collected from a Fenland marina and the whole rig headed north once again. Dobbin was almost on autopilot after these almost regular trips but still struggling with a performance deficit. On motorways the speed was embarrassing almost to the point of danger but on other roads I made frequent stops to allow following traffic to pass, hoping that this was accepted as good manners. 'Stay-awake tapes' of Rock and Roll music accompanied the plodding Dobbin and cargo and the driver was of course sustained by the cheese and Marmite sarnies.

But after the ubiquitous party and payment our friends at Badachro loaded Dobbin with a yacht to be delivered to Brightlingsea, nearly the other end of the country. The first few miles were covered quite easily but occasionally there was a feeling like a slipping clutch. This happened more and more frequently until finally, disaster struck. The lack of power meant excessive gear changes were necessary to climb the many hills and the clutch ultimately gave up. Thirty miles west of Inverness I managed to free wheel into a pub car park. If you have to break down it might as well strand you in a pub car park. But the pub, unfortunately, was closed and not just closed, it was boarded up. In due course a tow truck arrived from the Mercedes dealer in Inverness. The driver, a friendly cheerful chap attached a solid tow bar and subjected me to a terrifying white-knuckle ride back to the workshop.

White Knuckle Tow

The dealership was brilliant. The foreman even offered me a room for the night but I slept in the cab and enjoyed twenty-four hours exploring Inverness and made further investment in local products. Dobbin still struggled even with the new clutch and coupled with road closures due to bad weather, it took a further two days to reach Brightlingsea.

No party this time but the owner took me for a meal... and paid me. Dobbin struggled back to Hull and was put into intensive care. After all the hours of the so-called experts looking for the cause of Dobbin's breathlessness, the fault was finally identified. The throttle linkage was so rusty that instead of rotating under the floor, it twisted, thereby reducing the opening movement of the pump which was quite simply, starved of fuel. All that stress, embarrassment and frustration, all for want of lubrication.

After the throttle linkage transplant, Dobbin could really shift and we even found livestock on the windscreen; wasps, flies, moths and bees, some of them quite badly injured!

Look out you wildlife, Dobbin can really move!

CHAPTER FOUR
Tipped & 'Brassed Up'

Just as plankton comes near to the bottom of the food chain, consumed by those above, so HGV drivers and hauliers are the plankton of the supply chain and are similarly picked on by their commercial predators. Traditionally, an easy way to become invisible was to turn up at the Docks and present your Collection or Delivery notes. This would ensure that you would be ignored for several hours. As the power of dockers began to wane, 'Courtesy By-Pass' operations were performed on the staff of the Regional Distribution Centres of the increasingly powerful supermarkets or Cold Stores operated on behalf of the same pernicious organisations.

You could be penalised for being late, penalised for being early and generally treated with contempt. Having started at 'silly 'o' clock' you arrive at the security gate, a miserable security man lets you in, tells you where to park and where to present your notes and just to prepare you for the agonies ahead he casually remarks, "They're running a bit late this morning".

So you park up, don your high-visibility vest and join the queue of disgruntled drivers waiting to present their notes. Some of them are like you, new arrivals, looking moderately cheerful and optimistic. Others have that faraway look of despair and have straggly beards, grown whilst queuing and reflecting the time spent waiting. Eventually, a surly individual snatches your papers, glances briefly at them, then at you and sneers, "You're not booked in, there's no booking reference on your notes". He throws the notes back in your general direction.

"There's no booking reference on your notes", (repeated several times until you show him where the Booking Reference is clearly written).

"The product has the wrong code, there's no Order Number," he mutters (here we go again, show him the Order Number).

Then comes the all-embracing dismissal, "Get back in your cab; we'll give you a shout!"

There you languish for hours, unable to smoke, use your radio, unless you carry a spare key for they make you hand over your normal bunch, or use the 'facilities', which are reserved for the company's staff. This *"Period of Availability"* as it is now defined by the *Working Time Directive* means you are not at rest... true... and not working as such. You would like to be but you are incarcerated on alien premises, something like being locked up.

Conversely, and indeed *perversely, the Drivers' Hours Regulations* stipulate that for time spent not driving or doing 'other work' the driver must be free to dispose of his own time. No chance here! In short you are on edge, hoping you'll be called and expediently unloaded and with a bit of luck be tipped in time to finish the day's work which you were given in good faith. Eventually, you are released, possibly with the full delivery made but more than likely with a few pallets rejected for some spurious notion.

All the above reasons may be used to justify the rejection but one can be added, "Sell-by Date expired" to which you counter with the remark, "It was all well in date when I arrived here!"

Following on from this profit sapping behaviour, payment could take thirty, forty-five, sixty or even ninety days! One of the more repeatable phrases used about

Waiting in The Wilderness

supermarkets is, "They're making millions and busting thousands".

One of our agency drivers was married to a lady who worked for a finance company. Among their activities was the placement of funds on behalf of two of the big food retailers. Typically, money placed on Christmas Eve with the money markets would earn them around five million pounds each by New Year's Eve, but of course the suppliers of goods to those supermarkets would not be paid until the end of January or even later. It follows that suppliers and hauliers were unwittingly used as moneylenders. The catch-phrases such as, "Every Little Helps," "Saving You Money Every Day," or "Try Something Different," are nothing but cynical jokes for drivers and hauliers. Unless of course you are one of those high profile, publicity seeking green white and red operators who are now firmly wedded to the supermarkets in behaviour and culture.

What a contrast with boat transport! There is a

general rule on boatyards and marinas of "No Penny, No Pie". In other words payment up front or on the day of delivery or service. This is a very sensible and totally correct rule; when a job is done, payment is due. We have the absurd system in the UK where credit is taken, not freely given for days, weeks, months even years, benefiting none but the bankers, lawyers and big business. In General Haulage, the normal procedure believe it or not is for a small haulier or owner driver to sub contract to a larger haulier, manufacturer or more likely a Freight Forwarder. He will ask how much he is going to be paid and will be rebuffed with a curt, "We'll send you a Rate Con!" The 'con' stands for 'confirmation' but it might as well be another meaning of the word for he will have been tricked for sure. The rate given may be based on mileage, using 'AA' miles which shrink the country, or on time, weight, volume or the number of 'drops'. Imagine going into Currys, choosing a TV and as you leave the shop, saying to the salesperson, "I'll be in touch to tell you how much I intend to pay you". That's how it works for small hauliers. Then you wait and borrow money to 'tide you over,' extend the overdraft or survive by whatever means you have at your disposal. Meanwhile, your fuel supplier, if he gives any credit at all, will give you a fortnight at the most. Some help from the RHA and the FTA would be welcome.

    The marine industry seems to have seen the light, perhaps learning from bitter experience that goods remain in place until payment is made. The term 'cleared funds' is also a good watchword for a policy of ensuring that payment has really been made. Thus, through no particular business acumen on my part, it is almost always the case that upon completion of the job we are "Tipped and Brassed Up," meaning unloaded and paid! Nevertheless, the job is *very* competitive. It's only the cash-flow advantage that distinguishes boat transport from general haulage at least in financial terms. So, if you are a small haulier looking for a break in a niche market, please don't try to follow, there are plenty of us at it already.

The vexed question of VAT is often raised in discussions about our charges. Some can be very forceful, such as a guy who had agreed a price with me and 'rode shotgun' from Devon to Essex and whilst sat waiting for our escort I reminded him of the mutually agreed price. His response was as follows; "Listen Mayt, so far you've been a Diamond Geezer, so nao bleedin' VAT, bangers and mash in yer sky rocket, jamp on a playn, go git bronzed ap!"

Excuse the attempt to write in the correct accent; it was East End or Essex if the writing doesn't show it properly.

Every so often a new haulier springs up, does not charge VAT and lasts about six months. Apart from the vital need to claim back tax paid on fuel etc., it is impossible to operate a fully 'specced' artic below the VAT threshold. So these competitors do not last long but can do damage while they are around.

Insurance is a very expensive item and it's probable that non-VAT transactions and under the counter payments will mean there is no valid insurance especially for Goods In Transit cover. Whilst most of us resent paying taxes, or more to the point resent how taxes are spent, it is amazing that someone paying many tens of thousands of pounds for a boat will risk not being insured. I believe that we have the best cover available, but it does not come cheap. There is a correlation between the very wealthy who can easily pay whatever we ask but won't, and the ordinary hobby boater who trusts us to be fair and pays without question. In truth, very few people outside our industry have the slightest inkling of our costs and risks and those who do know, ask why we bother for such minimal returns! It is gratifying that most people are genuine and pay their bill with good grace. Thankfully, we have little bad debt which is fortunate because in this 'land fit for lawyers,' nobody can be forced to pay, whatever the law says. We have been lucky in this respect and generally work on the better nature of the individual rather than resorting to law.

Vehicle operating costs are of course astronomical and none more contentious than the cost of fuel. The protests in September 2000 were perhaps the last successful manifestation of 'people power', being more or less spontaneous and enjoying popular support. Rolling road-blocks and picketing of refineries were beginning to have an effect on society and just for once, the government took notice. People delayed in the road blocks were generally supportive of the action and there was a mood of common purpose.

The minister in charge of the nation's transport had proclaimed "Sack me if I fail", but then he's one of the 'untouchables' - the politicians, civil servants, quango kings and queens, union barons, health trust executives, local government officers, all members of the self-promoting, self-perpetuating 'Establishment' - who run the UK for their own mutual benefit and are often not sacked but promoted for failure!

Phew, that's a mouthful.

Anyway, back in September 2000 I was at a riverside marina in Yorkshire using a hired lorry just before we purchased Little Mandy. I was loading a cruiser to take to The Norfolk Broads and re-loading another one back. I took a call from Colin who owned and ran the most professional refrigerated transport business in the region. He told me the government had made a concession; that for the duration of the crisis hauliers would be allowed to use 'Red' diesel as road fuel. I was but a pipe's length from the red diesel bowser used to supply the boats on the river. The opportunity was too good to miss, so I filled up on 'Red', VAT-free and cheap. The following morning, I was back at the same place so topped up on 'Red'. Then Colin rang again with the revised edict from on high; "All use of 'Red' diesel must be recorded and declared to HM Customs and Excise. The outstanding duty would then have to be paid". Naturally. Of course.

CHAPTER FIVE
Mad Max Comes Home

In the autumn of our first year of boat haulage, the hired boats were returned to Hull. To celebrate the end of what they regarded as a fine season, our customers had a huge party. Despite having had just a few weeks' charter for the boats, the whole venture was deemed a great success and further developments would follow.

They had become a beneficiary of the largesse of the Highlands and Islands Development Board, a quango before quangos were famous, which had big lumps of public money to help fledgling businesses and keep the area populated. The HIDB had flown our Badachro boaters to the Southampton Boat Show to see what sort of yacht they would like for Christmas and helped them to purchase a Teliga yacht from Poland, which I collected from Brightlingsea.

Hey Ho! Another trip to Scotland.

The Teliga was added to the fleet. By employing a school leaver the charter business became one of the HIDB's favourite organisations in the region. I was more than happy to be on the fringe of this activity and rather hoped they would plan to do it all again the following year. Meanwhile, the last charter boat was prepared for its return home.

As this yacht was being loaded at Gairloch, Mad Max appeared with some extra cargo. He had four or five 'dressed lobsters' which were for consumption in England. They were not 'dressed' in the culinary sense, but in Max's T-shirts. He blocked up the drain slots in the well of the

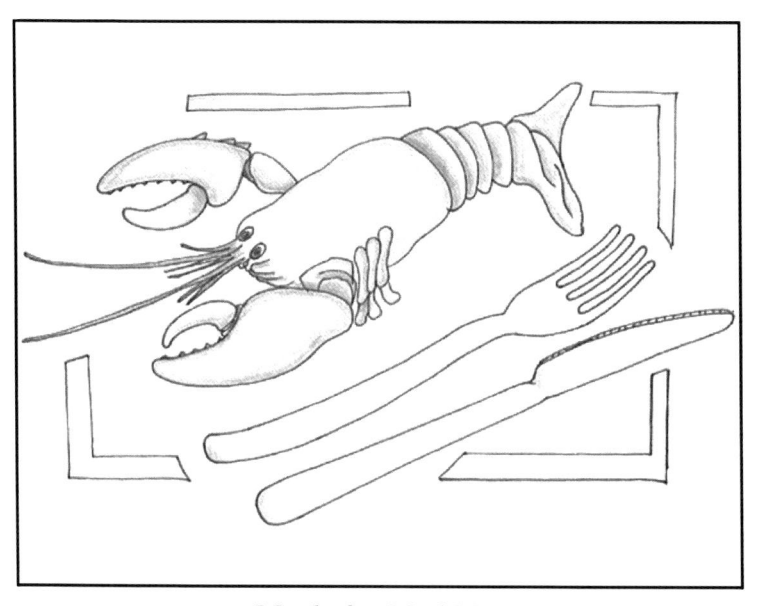

Meals for Mad Max

trailer and filled it with sea water. The wet T-shirts and the mobile pool would keep them moist, fresh and indeed active for the journey south. Who needs a guard dog when you've got a team of aggressive crustacea. They would become involved in a couple of incidents en route.

The Badachro boaters had chosen a pub in the next village for the party and everyone who had been involved in the charter business attended. A great atmosphere prevailed until Max tried to extract payment for his services during the season. They had fed, watered and accommodated him, in more ways than one, for over six months but there was a dispute over a cash payment. I did not get involved and never found out the cause or outcome of the argument but Max stormed out of the pub and was not seen again that night. He had a walk of over five miles back to the village, a journey the rest of us completed by car. It was apparent that our drivers would have been over the limit but there was a 'blind eye' surveillance from the local police at the time. The next day, hangover cleared and handshakes all round, I prepared to return to Hull.

But there was still no sign of Max. After searching the chalets and houses where he might have sought shelter the previous night he was eventually found asleep in the boat that we had loaded to take home. He would not be coaxed or enticed out of it. Perhaps he could have been bribed to disembark but nobody felt like trying that option, money being the cause of his self-inflicted isolation. He insisted that he would make the journey in the boat where he would be quite comfortable. I couldn't disagree, he'd certainly be more comfortable in the yacht being towed by Dobbin than being blown around in the sea. Despite my exhortations he would not come down so we set off. At least I would not have to share the sarnies, could smoke at will and enjoy my choice of music. By nightfall we had reached Dalwhinnie, a small hamlet on the A9 between Inverness and Perth, home to a superb, smooth malt whisky of the same name. At the time the village also boasted a truck-stop where we parked up. Max came down, showered, ate dinner and returned to the yacht.

"I'll be leaving at 5 a.m. Do you want to come down to ride in the lorry?" I asked as he climbed back aboard.

"No, leave me alone!"

Max clambered up the stern ladder, swinging somewhat dangerously before gaining a proper foothold and disappeared into the cabin.

As he left I said, "I'll knock on the boat and wait five minutes. If you don't appear I'll set off."

There was no comment to that and no response at four-thirty the following morning when I knocked on the hull of the boat. I stopped a little later at Kinross Services on the M90 and parked next to a coach that was disgorging a large party of ladies, or even a party of large ladies, into the restaurant. I joined the queue, purchased what was peddled as a breakfast and sat down. But before I had the chance of sampling it, a scream of terror split the air as the

Scary Max and the Lobsters

shocked ladies spotted Mad Max on the deck of the boat, sporting his attempt at contemporary motorway fashion. Looking around, stretching and scratching he was dressed in a one-piece undergarment, the ubiquitous sailor's cap and rigger's boots. The one-piece was like a 'babygrow' for grown- ups, not the fashionable modern item the 'Onesie'. It had not been washed for some considerable time and was seemingly the main item in Max's travelling wardrobe. Come to think of it, he had a strange resemblance to the drunken gunslinger in the film 'Cat Ballou'. I'm not sure what was the main cause of the ladies' anguish; Max's dishevelled appearance or the lobsters straining to get out of the trailer.

    He climbed down off the boat with the audience watching his erratic progress. Upon reaching the ground he marched into the restaurant and bought a cup of tea. He then poured the tea into a saucer, before slurping and swallowing it noisily, as the ladies watched aghast at the performance. When the teacup was empty, Max stood up, marched back to the lorry, climbed up onto the boat, scratched his important parts again and went below. The ladies, entertainment over, resumed their chatter and our journey continued with the same unsocial arrangement.

After passing York, we came across an accident on the A1079 at Kexby Bridge. A York bound livestock lorry had crossed the carriageway and crashed into some trees and several head of cattle were grazing by the roadside. Traffic heading to York was being diverted to Sutton in Derwent and we were being held back by an officer standing in the road. Obviously this took place back in the days when a policeman was prepared to stand in the road without a five-mile stretch first being coned off by the Health and Safety mafia or the Highways Agency Traffic Wombles. I was waiting patiently, first in the queue of east bound vehicles, with the brave officer but a few feet in front of me, when a voice boomed out, "Get a move on!"

The officer turned, looked accusingly at me, but I just shrugged.

"Get a move on, the tide's going out," the voice repeated, even more loudly and fiercely.

The officer glared at me again, then raised his eyes over the roof of the truck. There was Mad Max Griffin on the pulpit of the yacht, shouting and waving. Despite the probability that all sorts of offences were being committed and me expecting to be detained, the officer waved us through. I waited for Max to return below decks, waved a thank you to the kind officer and continued on the journey.

An exceedingly ungrateful and ungracious part of me wondered if our release was due to a problem that the officer would have had describing the scene in his note book.

"I was standing stationary on the carriageway of the A1079 between York and Hull when I was hailed by a sailor on the pointy bit of his boat demanding passage

Power gives way to sail

ahead. There were several lobsters nearby also behaving in a threatening manner!"

Whenever I see the blue and white sign at the side of the road saying, "Police Slow" I think, Yes, we know. Anyway, after that incident, the remainder of the journey seemed particularly uneventful.

We could perhaps have been prosecuted for breaking rules pertaining to livestock transport. The lobsters, complete with Max's shredded T-shirt, had survived the journey and were becoming somewhat restless. Max put a couple down in our garden, much to the chagrin of Katie, our West Highland Terrier.

Katie took to just about everyone, especially anyone with food. She once barked savagely at a renowned dog lover, the legendary Miss Forbes from the Ministry of Transport. We could not understand why, for it had never happened to any other visitor. Perhaps Katie had a sixth sense. Miss Forbes had come to see us about some infringement to our Operator's Licence conditions but she was so concerned about getting on the right side of the dog that whatever our misdemeanour had been, it was overlooked. Katie eventually calmed down and grudgingly allowed Miss Forbes to occupy a seat. Our Operator's Licence was not even discussed. Katie laid with head between paws, quietly grumbling to maintain the fear in the room and ready to resume the savagery at a moment's notice.

Katie now took a strong dislike to Mad Max, for the food he brought was unsuitable for dogs, being both alive and threatening. Max thought it great fun to go for Katie with a wriggling, clawing lobster in each hand. She backed away on this occasion but sought vengeance when Max came 'unlobstered' on a later visit. On the other hand Neville and Elsie cooked and enjoyed one of the much travelled crustaceans.

Max was consulted for many future journeys. Despite his somewhat controversial lifestyle and confrontational manner, he was a mine of information about boats. We had many adventures together and I will always be grateful for his help and freely given advice in the early days of our boat moving. He was a well-known character in the yachting world, famous or infamous according to your viewpoint.

CHAPTER SIX
Time To Get Serious

For a few months, jobs came along involving different types of boats and many new destinations. Life was pretty good. I usually had the time and opportunity to sort out the week's work for the regular drivers and arrange stand-by reserves for the last minute requests from customers. This sounds quite well organised and professional but it wasn't like that all the time. I tried to be organised or at least make it seem organised in order to justify my absence. So, equipped with fags, tea and a box full of cheese and Marmite sandwiches off I went.

It soon became apparent that boating was not confined to the wealthy and our coasts and inland waterways were awash, pun intended, with potential customers of infinite shape, attitude and income. I had to learn boating terms in order to appear knowledgeable.

"Oh yes, she's deep chined you know" or "Ketch rigged is she, super," or "No, she's on legs not shafts," or "Deck stepped, just fancy."

These phrases roll off the tongue to give a pretence of familiarity! But the single most noticeable feature was the general standard of courtesy shown to me as the driver. People saying "Please" and "Thank You" to a driver was a refreshing change, and a stimulus to expand these activities. These conditions are the exact opposite of those endured by most haulage operatives.

The trailer belonging to Mad Max's customer was borrowed, hired or commandeered for these jobs and the experience was invaluable but it became apparent that it was unsuitable for some vessels. A suggestion from Ron Linton, a friend of Max's and a local marine fibreglass expert, that a car transporter could be converted to accommodate boats proved to be an inspired idea. A 1973 Hoynor Mk7 was sourced, purchased minus its' top deck and the conversion commenced.

Now, let me state categorically, my engineering skills are zero. Indeed, simple DIY tasks are usually bodged or a complete failure. But failure or incompetence can sometimes have unexpected positive side effects. Many years ago, Angela was in hospital suffering from meningitis and her mother was en route from Leeds to help me look after Paul, then still an infant. I cannot offer any justification or explanation for this questionable behaviour but I thought I would freshen the place up prior to her arrival, so I emulsioned the kitchen ceiling. Yes I did, really. Elsie of course had spotted all the flaws in my efforts whilst still on Leeds Ring Road and pointed out these errors upon her arrival. Obviously, my work was not up to standard so I have never decorated since. Good result!

A more dramatic DIY event was my attempt to route a co-axial cable through a defunct gas pipe to bring television reception into the kitchen. On a sunny Sunday morning I drilled possibly the neatest hole I have ever done, perfectly round, not jagged or elongated and exactly in the right place. As I stared at the hole, admiring the absolute precision of the drilling and preparing to enlarge it with bigger drill bits, my plans were cruelly interrupted. A gentle hissing sound could be heard, which stopped when I put my thumb over the hole.

"Surely not a gas leak, that pipe has been isolated for years," I argued to cover my embarrassment. In fact the pipe was the main supply to the central heating and I had drilled into it, fortunately not causing a spark. The gas board emergency team duly arrived and commenced to assess the job. There were lots of derogatory comments, much pursing of lips and stroking of chins and an analysis of what was to be done.

"We'll need to replace six metres of pipe, that stuff hasn't been used for years."

"Aye, and that wall will have to be removed to give access to the meter and the mains supply." "We'll need to get bricklayers in too, to make good what we've chopped out."

"Can't do anything today, it'll need booking with t'workshops."

I thought it wise to remove myself from the discussion, being the cause of all this consternation, so I decided to take a pair of scissors to the overgrown weeds in the garden pond. After successfully thinning a patch of lilies, I moved onto the oxygenating plants and almost immediately came across some strong resistance!

Oh No! I was cutting into the cable which powered the pump and waterfall. I retreated without doing more damage and have never attempted any electrical tasks since.

Meanwhile, Angela was having none of this prevarication from the gas board team.

"Why can't you just put a blob of solder over that neat little hole?" she enquired sarcastically, fixing the main spokesman with a withering look. Angela can seriously maim and possibly kill with a withering look. And so it was that a blob of solder was put over my neatly drilled hole and there it has survived intact for many years. A gas board repair team was despatched to us on the Monday and after more buck passing and foot stamping it was agreed that the solder was good enough!

So, obviously I would not be any use at converting a car transporter trailer to one capable of carrying boats. A competent engineer was needed.

It is my contention that the best work and the best

Trailer One Project Centre

suppliers come by recommendation. Talking to a marine supplies firm in Hull and explaining our requirements a surprising but ultimately a fine choice to engineer the project was a village blacksmith, David Athey, of Garton on the Wolds, near Driffield in East Yorkshire. David spent many patient hours listening to the requirements for the trailer and then set about turning the ideas into reality. There is something genuinely conducive to productive activity, sitting around an open fire, drinking tea and drawing thoughtfully on pipe or cigarette. This was the Project Centre and David was able to translate my layman's ideas into a working machine.

One of the main criteria in loading a boat for road transport is to get the keel as low as possible onto the trailer. Car transporter trailers are already quite low and can be enhanced for boat transport by cutting the cross members and inserting a low well. This allows the keel to be set low down, reducing the overall height and increasing the stability of the load. David's skills

Forty Shades of Blue

transformed the trailer and added a variety of support systems to 'cradle' the boat and provide a comfortable, safe ride. Not being prepared to risk too much investment from borrowings, the final paintwork was completed by hand with volunteer labour including that of my "in-laws" who generously spent several afternoons at Garton, painting the trailer and indeed themselves. Elsie ended up with glossy blue hair, not just a 'rinse'.

The running gear on the trailer was a mixture of old and new; the very modern air suspension gave a comfortable, secure ride, but primitive cross ply *tubed* tyres severely limited the weight carrying potential of the vehicle. Subsequently, these items would be tested to their limits... and beyond! "Boat Trailer 1 or BT1 was thus brought into action during 1990. Around this time our business comprised three sets of activities. Modesty precludes the use of the term 'division' but we had an HGV/PSV Driver Agency, Refrigerated transport or Temperature Controlled Logistics to use the trendy terminology, and Boat Transport. If truth be told, probably only the driver agency ever made money and if I had had a mere smidgen of business sense, it could have made a lot of money. We employed twenty or so agency drivers on good pay and conditions and they in turn built up a good reputation for the company. But society was changing and drivers of the right calibre were hard to find.

Working with food, it used to be said, was likely to be profitable and up to the 1990s it was more or less true. People will always need feeding, whatever the state of the economy. We moved meat and poultry for quality customers but 'reefer' haulage, once one of the best sectors of road haulage, was being screwed by the increasingly powerful supermarkets. We had several contracts at different times and had up to five vehicles on dedicated supermarket work but although turnover increased, profitability dived.

It's true, "Turnover is vanity and profit is sanity."

When you are busy and the business is growing, you tend to think all is well, but the biggest growth item in our business was the overdraft, which became subject to increasingly onerous terms. So naturally I focused on the boat transport, the fledgling side of the business, which couldn't be ignored because it was so nice. The jobs took me to many lovely places, especially Scotland, where we met lovely people and got paid. Sometimes Angela's Dad, Neville, would join me as Second Man or Attendant. Like many people who climbed up into a lorry cab for the first time, Neville was impressed by the height, the status and the view.

"Ooh, you can see so much more from up here."

Compared to organising the drivers who each had their narrow agenda, compared to booking the fridge work where the customers made ever more difficult demands and compared to being in the office looking at the accounts with head in hands in despair, this just wasn't work.

I should have closed the driver agency, ceased the refrigerated haulage and concentrated on developing the boat movements, but instead, for too long, I merely played at it.

Much of the work was generated around Hull Marina, a development by Hull City Council and for a Labour controlled council, very progressive. Many derelict and redundant dockland areas around the country have been revived and rejuvenated by the arrival of recreational activities and Hull was one of the first.

Mad Max always held that people will always find money for leisure. Many years and many boat deliveries later I would have to agree. He and I struggled out of Tidemill Yacht Harbour at Woodbridge with a badly fire-damaged Princess 42. The exit is always difficult due to a building on a tight bend, made worse on this occasion by being clad in scaffolding. Having extricated ourselves, we called the police who required that we had an escort to the A14. Max decided to go walkabout and was missing when the police arrived. I ran round the village looking for him but failed to find him. Just as the police were about to abort the job, Max returned. Not for the first time, he antagonised our escorts. The delays left us stinking of charred wood and stranded at Colsterworth as night fell. Dobbin's accommodation was spurned for the chance of a shower and a bed at the Services. The boat was delivered the next day to Ron Linton for repair and refurbishment.

Spaces between groups of houses are variously called 'alleys,' 'ginnels' or in Hull, 'tenfoots'. There is therefore a gap of ten feet, which means a vehicle of around eight feet in width can comfortably travel through but probably requiring the mirrors folding in. So, loaded with a 9'6" wide yacht at Hull Marina, Max directed me to one of the famous 'Avenues' in the town and along a 'tenfoot'. The crane had squeezed in ahead and was ready to lift. At each pillar supporting the walls at the side of the alley, the boat had to be cranked away, then the lorry reversed a little and then the boat was cranked over the other way at the next pillar on the opposite side. This, a little local job, took most of the day. The boat was to be restored in the garden of a house. It may well still be there!

Max came with me to deliver another damaged boat, *Fine Art*, which went from Hull to Bangor in North Wales. This being before the privatisation of escorting and at a time when North Wales was receiving heavy investment in tarmac, the journey took a full two days. We calculated 42 police man-hours were involved in escorting us to Bangor, before leaving us stranded in an isolated part of the A55. The quest for a pub and some grub involved a long walk and some serious scrambling.

Eventually, Max went 'legit' and developed his skills as a small business venture. He remained a source of help to me while he repaired, valeted and sailed his clients' craft.

Dobbin and Trailer One were made for each other. Boats up to forty feet or so, that's twelve metres and a bit in new money, rarely weigh much more than twelve tonnes, or around twelve thousand kilograms, again in new money, especially those made of fibreglass. Some timber and steel craft might exceed these weights but most of our cargoes would be under ten tonnes, or even tons if you prefer the old spelling. With a bit of advertising and the recommendation by satisfied customers the boat work increased. It seemed to involve nice people, going to nice places and improving the cashflow of the whole business.

CHAPTER SEVEN
You Can't Do Enough For A Good Boss

In the early 1990s boat work increased either because we were cheap or perhaps we were establishing a good standard of service. I would like to think it was mainly for the latter reason. Either way I was increasingly 'playing boats' as it was scathingly referred to, often away all week. The weekends were spent catching up on paperwork. We had around twenty drivers on agency work of which the top five could be sent anywhere to do virtually any kind of driving, including: artics, tippers, reefers, bulkers, concrete mixers etc. The next ten were 'horses for courses', local work only for example, and the rest would be part timers who could fill in at night or at weekends. Certainly we had some excellent employees but in haulage, in the eyes of the competition and your customers, 'you're only as good as your worst driver'.

To be fair, over the years we had been fortunate to employ some first class drivers who sometimes appeared just at the right time, when fate for once played us a good hand. We used to say, "Once you've worked for BTS the only way is up" and many found further employment with our customers who had the benefit of having them on hire, able to evaluate them without long term commitment. Similarly, the driver had an incentive to do a good job if there was a chance of being taken on by one of our blue chip clients. Valued for more than their earnings, some of these lads quite simply made our reputation.

Stu' Brearley was a good example; one Friday afternoon the phone rang and Willerby Caravans asked if we could supply a driver on Monday with caravan transport experience. With our motto at the time, "Say Yes, and then wriggle," I agreed to send them a driver of the required pedigree. I hadn't a clue who to send and couldn't do that sort of work myself. About five minutes later the next phone call was from a chap who'd just returned from Australia as his wife couldn't settle there and he was looking for a job.

"What did you do before you went to Oz?" I asked.

"I worked for Willerby Caravans!" I kid you not, that's exactly how Stuart started with us, had six weeks moving caravans then graduated onto tippers, then was head-hunted by the tipper operator and subsequently became an owner driver.

It was a similar story with Steve Needham. Brought to our door by another driver as a shy twenty-one year old Steve developed into the ultimate agency driver. Wherever he was placed he did a thoroughly good job and was always requested as first choice by the customers whether it was for pouring concrete, delivering coffins or even driving coaches. He undertook every task that was put before him and gained a wealth of experience. In time, of course, he wanted better things so became an owner driver, first with an artic, then back to his favourite vehicle, a tipper on local work.

There were several other high quality drivers who worked for us and helped maintain and promote our business simply by doing a very good job. Some drivers turned up experienced and wary of agencies, not an unreasonable sentiment considering some of the outfits that were masquerading as professionals; 'Careless Hands', 'Drivers *R* Us' 'Skiver-drivers' and several more got the industry a bad name. We suffered a few 'odd bods' as well.

Her Majesty's Services have been generous providers of recruits to the road transport industry, generally equipping its members with a licence to drive at least a rigid HGV. The Services tend to build a culture of dependence, whereby orders are to be obeyed, routines executed without question, rules followed slavishly and any signs of initiative are frowned upon. In road transport, an industry dominated by rules and regulations, these qualities should be greatly appreciated and valued, but the culture causes frustration for drivers and employers alike.

John, who had been in the RAF and had gained some HGV driving experience since leaving, announced that he was the best driver I would ever employ! He was placed with a horticultural business delivering seedlings throughout the country. The routine was to load and run on a Monday, complete perhaps twenty deliveries, collect as many empty trays as could be found at each customer and return on Tuesday evening. Wednesday and Thursday would follow a similar pattern, leaving Friday available for a day run. The customer made two basic but crucial mistakes as John left the yard on the Monday morning. They gave him a computer printout of the presumed location of *all* the empty trays in the country and as he left the transport manager shouted, "Don't come back without a full load of empties!" To an ex-serviceman an order is an order, not a broad generalisation. Be aware that all this took place in the days before cellphones.

No sign of John on Tuesday when he was due back, or Wednesday when he should have been away with his second load, or Thursday. Our customer phoned his customers and established that John had done the deliveries in reverse order, a monumental task considering that the vehicle was loaded with eighteen hundred trays in a specific sequence. He had also been spotted in areas where he was not due to be delivering. His absence threw the whole business into turmoil. He finally arrived back on Friday afternoon wearing a smug smile of satisfaction that he had done a perfect job. He remained unruffled by the

Seedtray Check List

torrent of abuse that met him when he went into the office. Blissfully unaware of the chaos he had caused and totally confident of his own righteousness.

"You said, Don't come back without a full load of empties." He had dutifully worked his way through the 'Empties List', gone miles off route, walked from field to field in pursuit of his quarry and had brought back... a full load of empties!

Dave deserves space as a typical squaddie. Built like a gorilla, bounding with energy, confident about any task offered, totally lacking in patience, completely tactless, full of enthusiasm, undaunted by apparent problems, dismissive of difficulties, yet thoroughly honest and hardworking. The army had instilled a feeling of self-confidence and blind obedience no matter what situation occurred. It's not just the discipline, it also removes the thought process.

Ask an ex-squaddie to carry out any task and his reply will invariably be "No Problems" or the less convincing "No Probs."

Dave would utter this traditional response to any request even before the full instructions were given. He'd probably launch into a flashback of how he'd done this task before, probably under intense enemy fire, embellishing or outdoing every previous statement. He could cap anybody else's experiences, with the monologue beginning with, "When I was in the Daft and Barmy!"

He soon earned the title 'Rambo'. Even mundane jobs were transformed into multi-coloured epic adventures. A conversation on the CB radio whilst on local dock shunting would elicit a commentary such as this.

"Are you there Dave?" No Reply.

"Are you out there Dave?" No Reply

"Got your ears on Dave?" No Reply.

"Are you there Rambo, C'mon?"

"Who zat calling Rambo on the CB? Yo, I'm on the superslab, been to do a Cumbernauld changeover, put another card in at Beattock, changed connies on the dock and I'm off to do another!" Any law enforcement officer listening to Rambo would have a book full of confessions ready for throwing. Trying to impart some form of conformity was impossible.

"Dave, we've had a complaint about you driving through Brandesburton village too fast. What do you know about it?"

"Well, I'd got a tight deadline, had to ram it on in there, scared a few locals but I was only doing seventy. Anyway, who is complaining, maybe they'd like some hospital food?" Always cheerful, never one to complain, Dave wore out many pairs of boots - well the right ones anyway - while he was with us. He also wore out several trucks and one or two transport managers. Once and only once did I let him anywhere near a boaty type person. We'd gone to the Marina to pick up the trailer and he got in conversation with a yachtie who attempted humour by asking what happened if a boat fell off our vehicle.

Rambo replied on our behalf, "No Probs, we just kick it to the side of the road, ram it on in there and clear off!" Absolutely the wrong answer Dave. Eventually, when overwhelmed with debt, he spun and rolled his car, walked to the nearest pub, had a few pints and some chasers, phoned the police, accepted a DD conviction and enrolled at college for re-training. In one simple act he foiled his creditors, got the CSA off his back and robbed the haulage industry of a real character.

Sam, a Glaswegian, had left his home town many years ago but his accent was as strong and raw as if he had left only yesterday. He had genuine experience of all kinds of haulage work and could be relied upon to undertake anything. He soon built up a good reputation with clients who would ask the agency for Sam by name. Well, actually they would ask by many other names such as 'Jock', 'Haggis', 'That Scotch Git' or worse, but they really did want Sam. His willingness to work meant regular placements with quality customers. Frequent bumps and scrapes tarnished his reputation but Sam would always be ready with an excuse.

"I didn'a! I couldn'a! I hadn'a! were stock replies for damage and carelessness. Such was the vehemence of his denials that he generally got away with these little mishaps. He worked for us for many years and was eventually transferred to one of our customers. There he was affectionately or frustratingly called, "WM", "Wasna Me". Sam was a great worker of 'the old school'.

Peter, later to become our shop steward, had been a tyre fitter before joining us and was placed on contract delivering imported flat pack East German furniture nationwide, which suited him perfectly. Because most of the deliveries were to shops, early starts were unnecessary and they closed early too, so Peter could, and did, organise his hours of work 'to suit'. Our customer eventually noticed his self-established routine of mid-morning starts so issued an ultimatum that further tardiness would result in his removal from this work. We sent him a written warning that his lateness was putting the contract in jeopardy.

His reply included words to the effect, "I do not object to relocation but I cannot find Jeopardy in my Atlas" The contract ended soon after this as the East Germans were climbing over 'The Wall', a prelude to unification and they stopped making the cheap furniture.

Apart from his dislike of early starts, or perhaps the cause of his dislike of early starts, Peter liked his beer. I made a big mistake putting him on meat deliveries which meant Smithfield Market in the middle of the night. Peter took drink, got into an argument with the porters about the relative strengths of northern and southern beers, had a bump, got locked up and done for DD. The recovery of his vehicle was a fluke of good fortune as I was in London at the same time and managed to complete his deliveries and my own. The court case for Peter's offence was a revelation. It was held in London and Peter attended, resigned to his fate but hoping for a reasonable fine to go with the inevitable disqualification. The prosecution outlined its case, presenting the facts and reminding the magistrate of the seriousness of the situation when a professional driver is found to be 'over the limit'. The Beak suddenly interrupted and asked Pete who was representing him. Peter replied that he was just a poor northern lad and being riddled with guilt had come to take his punishment. He could not afford to employ a legal representative and did not wish to waste the Court's time. The magistrate asked to see Peter's licence and Peter handed it over.

"It's clean!" exclaimed the Beak "never seen one of these before".

Peter feigned embarrassment. The magistrate asked

Good Judgement

the prosecutor if the case was watertight, apparently becoming sympathetic. The lawyer replied that the case would be proven but he too wished to help Peter. There was a short adjournment while legal terms were discussed and upon resumption the prosecutor swapped roles to defend Pete.

"With your permission m'Lud I will speak on behalf of the defendant". He outlined six items of proof required to secure a conviction but added that he could only be sure of five and a half of them!

"Please explain," said the magistrate, warming to the situation.

"Well, The Defendant's breath showed excess alcohol, his urine sample was neat beer, the blood tested positive, the defendant was on the public highway and had been instructed to move by a market porter and he collided with a car".

"Which bit do you consider was only worth half?" asked the puzzled Beak.

"The motorist shouldn't have been there in the first place!" asserted Pete's self-appointed Brief.

"That'll do for me," said the Beak, preventing the lawyer from changing his mind or reverting to his role as prosecutor, "the Defendant will stand and receive sentence. Young man, I'm going to show you all about southern justice!"

Peter braced himself for the inevitable, but sounding like a market trader in reverse, the magistrate boomed out his imaginary wares.

"I'm not going to send you to prison, I'm not going to disqualify you from driving, I'm not even going to fine you. You are free to return to your home in the North with your licence and reputation intact!"

Peter wondered if he dare ask for the refund of his train fare but decided not to push his luck. He carried on driving, oversleeping and drinking.

Jack Motley was 'old school', loyal, hard-working and utterly reliable. He also grew the best tomatoes you've ever tasted on a home brewed fertilizer whose ingredients he declined to identify. He preferred local work so that he could keep an eye on his allotments and was well respected by all our customers. He was taken from this world too soon having just reached retirement. His produce would surely have flourished if only he had been granted the time. Many years on we still hear from June his widow.

Charlie, who I always referred to as 'Man In A Suitcase' because of his resemblance to the TV character of that name, stood out from the popular conception of a lorry driver. He was smart, wearing overalls he provided himself, he was punctual, his paperwork was immaculate and his timesheet was always handed in on time, beautifully presented. In short, he was the ideal agency driver. He was in great demand for his pleasant, willing, hard-working manner and it was difficult to know where to send him, as most of the customers requested him by name. Nothing was too much trouble.

One Saturday morning he brought his time sheet, punctual and precise as ever. He asked to be released without notice as he wanted to join a relief convoy taking supplies to Eastern Europe as Communism was collapsing. I could hardly refuse such a noble request.

The following Monday evening the police arrived with a strange tale to tell. On the previous Friday, Charlie had been involved in an accident in one of our customer's vehicles. Ordered to take his documents to his local police station as was the procedure, he confessed to having no licence, could not read or write and said that he would be moving away from the area. The officer produced documents relating to over four hundred offences since leaving school! Most were for fraud, deception or embezzlement. How had his licence, or lack of it, slipped through our procedures? He had admitted to the police that his landlady completed his time sheet each week. What would happen to us and to the customer whose lorry was involved? The trust between our business and our customers was shattered. I went cap in hand to explain the events to all those who had hired him and hoped that the damage would be limited. The aftermath was enlightening.

No fewer than three of our customers were considering hiring him and had been fooled by his license ploy! Nobody would believe our story and he was soon after seen as large as life in local hauliers' vehicles. So what happened to the police action? We shall never know.

Another likely lad with a question mark over his licence was a young Australian, brought to our door by his English girlfriend, a barmaid called Penny. Chris had family locally but needed to work to maintain himself. Once we had confirmed the validity of his licence he was put to work with several of our agency customers, usually taking Penny with him to help him find his way around the UK. Penny had obviously undertaken to give more than just Geography lessons, for whenever the vehicle stopped the cab curtains closed and the cab went into a frenzied rock and roll routine. Various items of underwear were recovered from the cabs by the regular drivers returning to their vehicles. The comments of the customers who observed these antics varied from envy to disgust but there was no doubting the strong work ethic of our Commonwealth recruit. Chris had to be restrained from working day and night as he thought the drivers hours' regulations were a severe encumbrance and were to be ignored. The couple eventually set off for Australia, but have since split up and in the meantime Chris is sharing in Australia's resources boom, shifting coal.

There is a saying, "It wouldn't be a show without Punch", or the main man, call him what you will. Neil Quarterman became so well established in this business that some, and sometimes he, could believe that it was *his* business. He started as an agency employee, became adept at all types of work and was regularly requested by our customers who knew he would do the job properly. However, as our own vehicles needed 'jockeys' it was foolish to send the best ones out on agency work, even though that would make money whilst haulage invariably did not. So Neil was thus mainly on one of our own vehicles.

Our refrigerated vehicles were running seven days a week and one, nicknamed "Effbat" was covering seven thousand kilometres every seven days. But pressures and tensions were building up in the business. It was a period of aggressive bank behaviour and our financial position was becoming ever more precarious. The overdraft was extended on ever more onerous terms and eventually we put the house up for security. 'Directors Guarantees' they call it, definitely a move of utmost desperation and not to be recommended, a safety net for the bank. But I still managed to sneak away moving boats, convincing myself, if nobody else, that my efforts were helping the business.

One day, after loading a Birchwood TS37 at Port Edgar - yes, Scotland again, under the Forth Road Bridge - a worrying event took place. Mobile phones could be installed in vehicles but were as yet too cumbersome for the pocket. Answering what I thought was the first call of the day as we joined the A1, it was a very irate Angela demanding to know why I hadn't sent a driver to one of our best agency customers.

"Because they haven't asked for one," I responded.
"Dale rang you and you said you'd ring back!"
"No he didn't!" I replied.
"Yes he did and he's getting impatient!"
"I'm sure he didn't call me."
"Yes he did, shall I send Keith?"
"Who is Keith?" I enquired, not recognising the name of one of our drivers.
"Leave it to me; all you want to do is play boats!" Angela snapped and slammed the phone down.

I had a list of employee's names and phone numbers on the engine hump beside me and I asked the second man to read them out. I didn't recognise most of them. Angela, as on many occasions held the fort and sorted the problem.

Talk about panic! If part of the last hours activities were already forgotten, had I also made loading errors and just carried on? Had I strapped down the load? Had I left a trail of destruction behind? Looking in the mirrors didn't help. All that was visible was the lump of the boat. Somewhat apprehensively, after stopping to check the load, I carried on.

We parked at Thirsk that night, had a pub meal and a couple of pints. Back in the bunk I lay thinking about the day's events. I recalled Dale's request, the promise to phone back and the subsequent conversations. I could even remember the drivers' names.

Arriving back at the yard next day there was a deputation; Angela, Paul and the in-laws all demanding that I take some action. Reluctantly, I agreed to do less driving, spend more time in the office and try to run the job properly. Secretly, I thought, let the heat die down, develop new systems for the day to day running of the business and I could soon be away 'boating' again.

But two more incidents changed the game forever.

"Good Morning Doug, its Geoff, can I have a driver this afternoon please?"

Panic! I could not remember who Geoff was but somehow knew he spoke as an important customer. I stalled for time, promised to ring back and tried to collect my thoughts. Within half an hour, memory restored, I was able to comply with his request. Of Course, it would be the Geoff from one of our premium customers. Phew, that was a close call!

The final straw was a domestic incident.

One Saturday morning, no excuses accepted, Angela dragged me round town to buy a fire for the 'snug', a room which doubled up as our office and our 'telly' room. After indifferent receptions from some electrical shops we eventually made the purchase, came home and installed the fire. Later, as I took a bath, Angela came in for a chat, the bathroom being the only room where there was no phone. Free to talk, we ran over the day's events with Angela sat on the loo.

"The fire was a bargain after all the early hassle and disappointment, wasn't it?" said Angela.

"What fire?" I replied, the mind blank to the day's events; the shopping trip, purchase of fire and subsequent activities. Not the correct answer. It was time to see a doctor.

I will always regard these events as a safety valve for

the release of stress brought on by the hard work of running the business and the anxiety caused by the policies of the bank. However, it seems that stress is a state, recognised as a genuine medical condition only if you are a public servant of some kind. A teacher finding things too hot in the classroom; have a term off. A local government worker or civil servant feeling abused by being asked to do a full day's work; just drop out for a while and get some counselling on the rates. Best of all be a policeman, have a couple of dodgy arrests, get early retirement, but then come back to a desk job when you need a bit of a financial top-up.

But make your living by professional driving and your stress is imaginary; you must instead be epileptic, diabetic, neurotic and suffer from strokes or heart defects. Worse still if you make your living as a driver *and you smoke*, then you are nothing short of a criminal.

The results of various tests were inconclusive but an added factor was that as we paid into private health insurance the medics had almost a duty to find something wrong, thus perpetuating their lucrative employment. The outcome was serious.

"Stop smoking and have an aspirin every day!"

The aspirin thing was acceptable but to deny the bloodstream of nicotine was, to say the least and to say it with a modern ungrammatical phrase, a bloody big ask! Non-smokers cannot comprehend these sentiments but smokers looking back through life have fallen out with friends, fallen out with family, suffered from bad food, even worse from drink, but nicotine has never let them down. Stopping smoking is like losing a lover and there is nothing to replace her.

"Once a smoker, always a smoker".

The effort this time would last about a month, a month of misery. It would be another ten years before the conditions were right to live with nicotine deficiency. But even then, not until the harmonica blowing, Tunnocks Tea Cake munching, nicotine withdrawal system was available... Enough of the self-pity, what about the boats!

Step forward Neil Quarterman, 'Admiral Q' or just 'Q'.

Neil Quarterman had already worked for us for several years, originally forging a great reputation as an agency driver and by now a kind of unofficial road foreman on the 'milk'. This job was the biggest single contract we have ever had and was later almost to cause the downfall of the whole business. We served a dairy, delivering milk to supermarkets throughout the north of England. Neil would organise the loading of the trailers at the dairy and allocate the journeys to the other drivers. He had covered the more unusual jobs that came our way through agency work and before joining us was on tree-logging work. His experience and adaptability would now be invaluable. I asked him if he fancied trying the boat job and he enthusiastically agreed.

First, he needed to be acquainted with the procedures for loading and securing the vessels. 'Q' and I travelled to Mayflower Marina at Plymouth to load a Trader 41, a trawler yacht to bring back to Hull. I had incorrectly named the starting place on the route notification but the Devon Abnormal Loads Officer was helpful and allowed us to proceed from Mayflower. This would normally involve the coning off of Richmond Walk to prevent parking as the street is narrow and has some tight bends but this had not been done on this occasion due to my inaccurate application. However, two motorcycle policemen arrived to escort us out of town. I'll never know why but one of the hoist team on the marina took one look at the police, dived into the mess hut and stayed out of sight until we left.

Talk about 'Good Cop Bad Cop!' The first removed

his helmet and said, "I need a cup of tea, somewhere to pee and time for a smoke before we set off". He was, of course, obliged.

Bad cop says, "The job's stopped for twenty-four hours while the street is coned off and the correct notification is applied".

Good cop has a go about bad cop and we expected an end to our plans. Eventually, bad cop sulks off and sits astride his bike at the top of the street while good cop helps us to navigate around the obstructions and bounce a couple of parked cars onto the pavement. We emerge safely and are escorted to the A38. Bad cop has disappeared. Good cop stops while we re-check the load, has another smoke and then leaves us to make our way north.

The next few comments and observations would demonstrate a facet of 'Q's character which would manifest itself quite a few times over the years. As we travelled up the M5 it was almost dusk and in those days abnormal loads were not permitted to travel in darkness. We were approaching Sedgemoor Services, 'Q' was driving and I said, "We may as well stop here tonight".

No response.

A little louder I said, "We may as well stop here for the night."

Still no reply but Neil's face creased into a pet lip and he stared straight ahead. I knew he had heard me so I tried to be more assertive.

"We'll stop here for the night, pull in now!"

"This place isn't even open at night so there's no point stopping here!" was Neil's grumpy reaction. My next comment threw him into a tantrum.

"We'll take a walk out of the service area."

He nearly choked and bust a blood vessel as he spluttered, "These legs are meant for pressing pedals not for walking, we are not stopping here!"

These legs are meant for pressing pedals

"Pull up now, we are going for a walk!"

With great reluctance and exceedingly bad grace Neil parked up and with a continuous barrage of abuse we washed, changed and set off along a lane out of the service area. By now it was almost pitch black and we made our way along a country lane towards Brent Knoll, a small hill rising out of the Somerset Levels. Ignoring his constant moaning I led the way. Within ten minutes or so we approached the village of East Brent, nestling at the bottom of the Knoll. I think 'Q' believed I might have been about to ask him to climb it, when suddenly his expression changed. A building some way ahead had an illuminated sign on the wall.

Could it perhaps be, yes, it is the answer to his prayers, a pub. The face so creased and pained lit up with a smile and the legs designed for pressing pedals propelled him forward at a rate of knots! (That's a nautical term for speed, don't you know, seeing as how we are now in the marine world!).

As we entered the pub, the landlord frowned. "Oh dear", he said, "I still haven't got any!"

My revitalised companion looked puzzled. I had called here previously and been involved in a discussion with the landlord about the merits of different brands of malt whisky. He only sold Glenfiddich, very popular but not to my taste and I had extolled the virtues of Glenmorangie a consistently wholesome, warming brand. Having explained the conversation to Neil, we drank and dined, putting the Admiral 'Q' in fine fettle.

'Q' had undergone a transformation. Not only had he now become a boat mover, he had also become a *walker*, but only in the quest for escape from the inequities of motorway service areas. Thereafter, 'Q' was the pioneer of the discovery and patronage of off-site pubs, a much-needed facility to ease the pain of parking on Motorway Service Areas. Within a few months he had located, *walked to*, and tried out pubs near to many motorway service areas. If 'Q' said they were within walking distance, they certainly were! His first discovery set the pattern for future exploration. His first brave venture resulted from running out of hours on the M1.

M1 Watford Gap

Leave by service road on northbound side or cross over from the southbound side. The transport lines here represent three centuries of transport evolution. The M1, the LMS railway and the Grand Union Canal lie side by side. Cross the railway line and the canal to a site that was originally a cattle station for animals being sent to London by barge; hence the name of the pub, Stags Head. This pub, owned by a Portuguese family served superb bar meals and also had a restaurant. Now it's a Chinese restaurant and bar, still an excellent diversion less than half a mile from the motorway. This was Neil's first discovery of a pub near a service area and there is probably a plaque on the wall to recognise his achievement.

M1 Northampton (formerly known as Rothersthorpe) Services

Following Neil's public spirited example I set out from the park to find a pub. I walked for miles and miles on the east side of the motorway and had I gone due east, I would have walked far enough to have gone right through Northampton. But foolishly I had taken a lane in a north-easterly direction which led nowhere. Arriving back at the services, exhausted and parched, I should have just called it a day but I thought it might have been worth a quick look in the other direction. After about three hundred yards, there it was, a lovely pub with mock tudor beams and panels. In several of the spaces on the walls were charcoal drawn caricatures of various people identifiable as the barman, landlord and others in the room. Apparently the artist was able to pay for his beer by drawing a member of staff or a customer. Oh, to be possessed with such a skill. I half expected to find a sketch of Admiral 'Q' to prove he'd been there before me. Too late for food but thirst at last slaked.

M1 Leicester Forest

If northbound leave by the service road, take care because it runs next to the exit slip, then cross by the motorway bridge. If southbound just walk up the service road. A short road leads to the pub, passing on your left a house where they collect Hillman Avenger cars, yes really, and on the right where they collect electric milk floats, or maybe it's a dairy. The pub, The Forest Park is now a Premier Inn, boil in the bag stuff but better than motorway grub anytime. If you get stranded further north on the M1, try to avoid **Tibshelf.** It's miles to the nearest pub which doesn't do food and is probably shut by now anyway. The area around **Woolley Edge** has not been fully explored but no pub has yet been discovered. Still on the M1, **Woodall** has a nearby sanctuary but care is needed on a dark night as the lane to the pub is not illuminated and once you've escaped from the service area there are no footpaths. If northbound, cross to the southbound area and leave via a footpath that passes near the fuel pumps. Join the lane running south-eastwards and about half a mile up a hill the pub welcomes you.

M5 Gordano, another inspired discovery by Neil, was at a place frequently on our route and until recently one of the best places to park. The site operators allowed parking at the rear of the site where a steep mound had been built to keep the customers in. But, armed with some local knowledge, one night Neil was over the mound and across a field into the village itself and enjoyed the pleasures of a great English pub, the King's Arms, with guest beers and excellent food. The site operators have recently identified the 'leakage' of people and stopped truck parking near the mound. Gordano has gone from one of the best sites to one of the worst.

Similarly, **M5 Michael Wood** has recently destroyed what was once a good lorry parking area with access to a pub and restaurant, The Pepper Pot, near the south bound service road.

M5 Exeter Services provides not only a good walk but a series of hazards on the way to the pub. Take the A376 towards Exmouth but be careful of the 'traffic-light grand prix' starts on each leg of the roundabout. Cross this road at your peril and follow the unclassified road towards Topsham. Your reward is the Blue Ball, with fine food and ales but beware the midges in summer.

The **M27 Rownhams** has one of the best areas for parking of abnormal loads and is within striking distance of the marinas in and around Southampton. Proceed south of the services along a reasonably lit road through a housing estate and down a hill. There at the traffic lights, a choice of pubs with music, laughter and good food, ingredients not supplied by 'Road Thief'.

It crossed my mind to approach Collins or Philips to

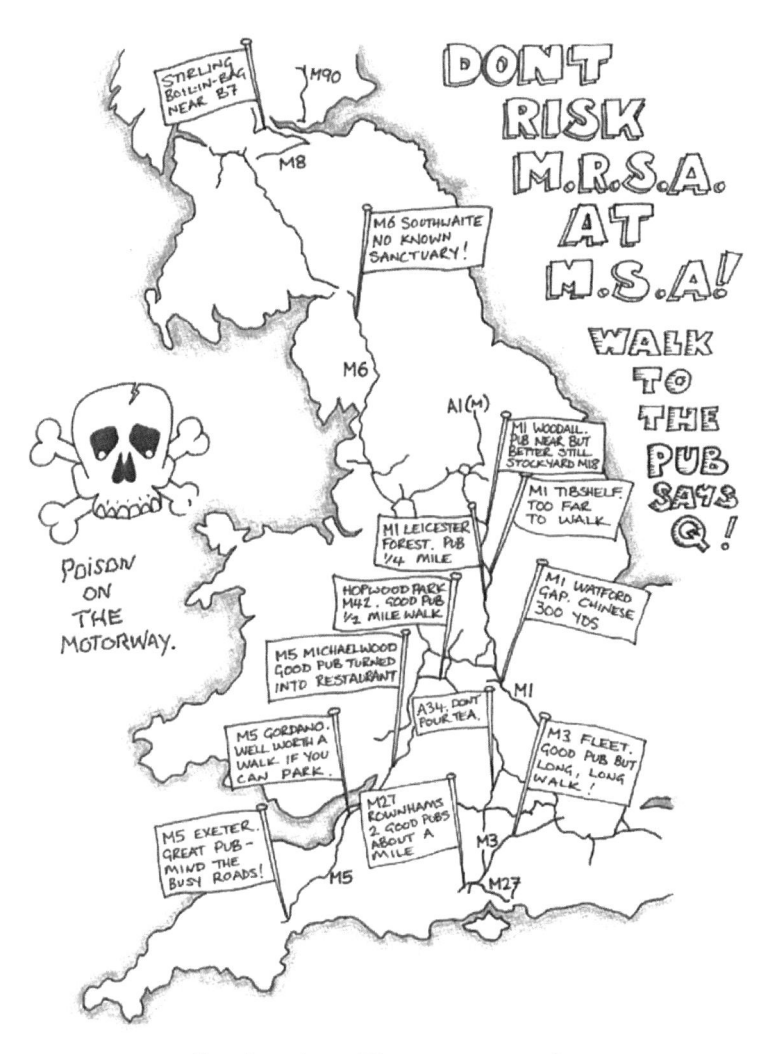

Service Area Escape suggestions

suggest the idea of inserting a page in their Atlas's showing the location of these oases of hospitality. I also considered submitting a page to show 'Roads where it was safe to pour tea on the move', and with a special colour code where it was safe to pour tea in a Scania without the beverage hitting the cab roof!

Fortunately, with the passage of time, night moves of abnormal loads, far from being prohibited, are positively encouraged where road conditions are suitable.

Even before the licenced thuggery imposed by some companies, under the guise of 'service area management', parking on these sites for the night was an indignity to be avoided if at all possible. Abnormal load bays were, and still are, normally occupied by selfish drivers having a short break and are rarely available to abnormal loads such as boats, mobile homes, combine harvesters or other big lumps that are entitled to use them. Furthermore, if you asked a site operative to remove the offenders from the Abnormal Load Bay, he was suddenly only using his blind eye. The food at these areas was abominable, showers virtually non-existent or out of order and there was no alcohol served.

'Q' took over the role of boatman and built up a fine reputation for customer service, developing that side of our business until two vehicles could be employed.

As he is often heard to remark with some irony, *"You can't do enough for a good boss!"*

CHAPTER EIGHT
Boats & Boaters

Boat owners are generally lovely people and we have come to regard many of our customers as friends. There is a perception that people with boats are 'wealthy buggers' as indeed some are, but many are quite normal and some even behave in a sensible cooperative manner. From our point of view the customer base can be roughly divided into three groups, with many sub-divisions.

Commercial operators obviously use their boats to earn a living. Owners of motor cruisers from the super-rich down to the hobby boater use their boats for pleasure and recreation, while the 'Flag and Stick' brigade regard themselves as the only true mariners, revelling in the pain, punishment and discomfort of yachting.

In the commercial group we find mainly fishermen. But increasingly marine contractors such as vessels serving the off-shore industries like oil and gas production, harbour authorities and recently the operators of off-shore wind farms provide a significant amount of work. We, in road transport like to think we suffer hardship but it is nothing compared to the deprivation and danger endured by fishermen. Dealing with fishermen is generally a straightforward affair. If they are about to buy a boat they will probably be buying a licence, a permit to fish and a quota to go with it. Yet they are hindered, hassled and hampered at every step and turn! How can it be that people willing to go to work - there are few enough of them these days – and suffer great hardship and danger, can be restricted to just a few days gainful activity in a year while foreigners can fish in UK waters with impunity. The Common Fisheries Policy is even more absurd than the Common Agricultural Policy. A quirk of fate got us onto the 'Find a Fishing Boat' website. Fishermen have been great customers and we try very hard to accommodate them even at short notice, but more about fishermen later.

Among the talents required for the driver of a boat transporter, the most vital is the delicate skill of loading the craft onto his vehicle. True, the driving process must be steady, progressive and very considerate for the boat and other road users. Whilst most crane or hoist drivers are patient and helpful, it inspires confidence in the customer if the operation is seen to be quietly efficient. Too much screaming and shouting suggests fear and doubt. Experience brings increased competence and the loading becomes a smoother, quieter operation. But even after many years, loading is still a time of intense nervous concentration with many simultaneous operations to watch, adjust and respond to. In the early days, loading was a particularly anxious time, as new and different types of keels and hulls were encountered.

Eventually, in theory at least, knowledge of a particular boat would enable the trailer to be set up according to its known characteristics. Little tricks would evolve to make the loading simpler and the journey more comfortable for the boat. Boat hauliers have always been adaptable and ingenious in making their trailers suitable for the task. It may cause alarm to suggest that the most likely equipment used for supporting your boat is an item purloined from the construction industry. In fact the "Common Acrow" is more likely to be incorporated into boatyard cradles and boat trailer supports than any other component. These devices are adaptable, flexible in operation, capable of being strengthened where necessary and above all, relatively cheap. It is a fairly simple process

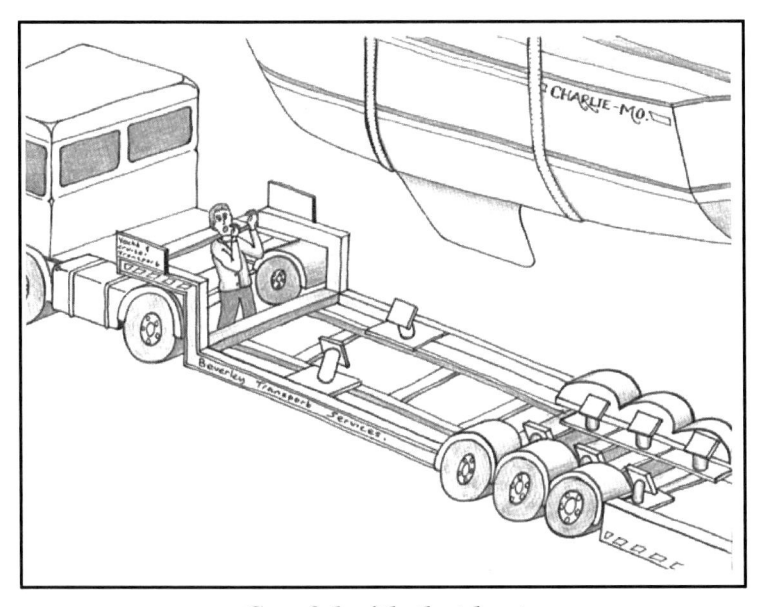

Careful with that boat

to add flat plates to the Acrows, cover them with rubber and carpet and fit the whole structure to the trailer, thereby creating a strong adjustable cradle, more or less a 'catch all' system.

For a while, we could replenish our stocks of carpet pieces used for insulation by a visit to the local carpet shop. Here, in a corner was a pile of neatly stitched samples and for a donation to the tea fund, we could fill the van up. I used to try to impress customers by selecting single colour samples and using them with nautical correctness, 'red' for port and 'green' for starboard! The carpet sales industry soon cottoned on to the re-cycling potential of these items, started charging, first of all at a fiver for an armful, then fifty pence each, then even more. We now resort to collecting off-cuts from shops or re-use our own carpets. Whilst this leaves our own homes with bare boards it means our customers' boats are comfortably pampered and insulated.

Our first trailer had a combination of Acrows, chains

and bottle screws to become the padded supports of the cradle. The bottle screws were left dry as oil or grease could have blown onto the boat when travelling at speed thus spoiling the surface. When loading at Hull one day a particularly inquisitive bystander, nothing to do with the boat being loaded, was getting in my way, disrupting the loading process, fiddling with anything that he could get his hands on, and generally being a nuisance.

"Why don't you oil these things?" he enquired, feigning difficulty in turning a bottle screw.

"Cos the boat would get splattered as it travelled along!" I snapped, working round him as he fiddled and twisted. He found something else to comment on. Noting that he was behaving like a yacht owner and me being the clever salesman I thrust one of our business cards into his top pocket.

"Why not try sailing in Scotland?" I shouted. "It's nice up there!"

I meant that he should perhaps go there immediately. He skulked away at last leaving me to complete the loading without his supervision. I felt a little concerned that I had been a bit rude, but I shouldn't have worried as a week or so later the phone rang.

"Hello, it's Jim, we met last week, I'm going to take your advice about sailing in Scotland, and so could you take my yacht to the Clyde please?"

Thus we moved "Bozo" a fin keeled yacht with a reputation for speed, once from Hull to Largs and again some years later when he had the audacity to bring it back from Scotland by water!

But first, the maiden voyage on the back of a lorry to Largs, a marina built from scratch with excellent facilities in beautiful surroundings on the Lower Clyde. Arriving at sunset with "BOZO" I was met by a friendly dockmaster who welcomed me and the boat, directed me to safe parking, and indicated the location of the showers, bar and restaurant. He apologised for being unable to unload me that night but promised me a 'lift-off at eight o' clock in the morning'.

What a contrast it was to Dockland, Cold Store or Supermarket, where the reception would be something like; "You're not booked in, you'll have to wait, go back to your cab and we'll call you when we can be bothered and No, you can't use our toilets or canteen and we just don't care if we make you late for your next delivery."

There have been literally hundreds of occasions when I have thought something along these lines; I'm here on the banks of the Clyde looking at the beautiful Isle of Arran. I could be sat waiting at Iceland Frozen Foods at Deeside or Tesco at Doncaster with no view, no civility from the staff, no chance of a quick turn round, in fact no hope! Boat transport is indeed a privilege.

We moved "BOZO" again some years later when the owner tried a DIY escapade that went wrong. First of all he'd had the affrontery to sail the boat back to the Humber instead of providing me with another trip to Scotland. Then he embarked on a caper with a homemade trailer and a VW pick-up, provided and driven by a mate as a favour, with the intention of taking 'Bozo' to his engineering workshop near Sheffield.

"Doug, it's Jim from 'Bozo'. I'm in trouble, can you help? I made my own trailer to move the boat but it doesn't work. The crane lifted Bozo out of the water, lowered it onto my trailer, but then the back went down and the front went up, lifting the towing vehicle off the ground. The boat is hanging there, the crane can't put it down and we're stuck until we get a proper trailer. Please hurry"

"Where are you?" I enquired.

"Grimsby Docks."

"Well, can't the marina help you?"

There was a fledgling marina on Grimsby Fish Dock,

D I Y Trailer Recovery

now a thriving organisation but then just a small club.

"I'm not at the marina, the lads on the bulk handling quay offered to lift the boat for a few quid in the hand. They are a bit impatient to get on with their own work but my boat is stopping them so you must come now."

"I will come as soon as there is a unit back to pull the boat trailer. 'Bozo' is over eleven-foot wide. Have you notified the police?"

One definition of an 'abnormal load' is one exceeding nine feet six in width and the police have to be given two days' notice of the move including the dimensions, weight and proposed route. Jim had not notified them.

"I will ask for a short notice dispensation and hope the police will agree."

Most Abnormal Load Officers are amenable to late notice applications providing it is not a regular request and we have always tried to establish and maintain goodwill with all Forces. Some can be totally inflexible but on this occasion both Humberside and South Yorkshire agreed to our journey. A good record of compliance has enabled us to be granted Dispensations with most Forces in the intervening years.

The first unit back was 'Slug', another unit from the same stable as Dobbin, obviously named for his dynamic performance. Slug was not really suited to pulling the boat trailer, but 'needs must' as they say, and time was running out. It was early afternoon on Friday by the time I set off for Grimsby and when I entered the bulk handling quay the dockers were ready to be knocking off. 'Bozo' was craned off the toy trailer, which returned to ground level and on to ours. Jim was obliged to ride in the lorry as his pal, by now perhaps his ex-pal, sped off somewhat aggressively with the pick-up and toy trailer. By then it was late afternoon and the dockers had gone home, locking the gates behind them. We managed to lever one gate off its hinges and make enough space to get out.

It is our practice to stop at intervals to check the security and safety of the load. As I pulled into the first lay-by on the A180 Jim asked why we were stopping. When I explained the reason he scoffed.

"If you'd loaded it properly in the first place you wouldn't need to keep stopping!" said the man who had just been rescued from his own incompetence. I kept quiet. I have long held the view that if you set out to write a piece of fiction about road transport, you couldn't dream up the things that actually happen.

The A180 becomes the M180 and at the end of this motorway we should have been able to join the M18 to go south. This motorway was closed due to a chemical spillage, an event designed to create maximum chaos on a Friday afternoon. The police were diverting traffic along minor roads and as it was now dark, this was somewhat hazardous with the wide load. In those days, abnormal loads were not allowed to travel in the dark. Slug had no beacons so we were not able to warn on-coming traffic about the extra size of the boat. I became so alarmed at this that I asked the police stopping traffic from accessing the motorway if I could go past the cones and wait for daylight in safety. Fortunately, the officer was sensible and helpful. He allowed us onto the motorway as we were south of the spillage but wouldn't let other traffic go through as they could have tried to go north in the other direction. For two or three junctions we had the motorway to ourselves. Jim was subdued and contrite.

"I'll never try this sort of thing again. I didn't realise there was so much involved or how it could all change and go wrong."

The nightmare was still not over. At Jim's workshop there was a roof mounted crane. Would you believe, it couldn't quite lift the boat high enough to clear the axles of the trailer? Eventually, against all safety regulations the boat was swung to and fro with ropes to raise it a fraction higher than the crane could achieve and on the upswing I drove away! It was nearly midnight and nearly bust on 'Drivers Hours'.

David Arnold was very much a product of the 80s; making big money and spending it fairly ostentatiously. Given to snapping orders and leaving his PA to sort out the details he would not accept rejection or delay. He was, however, a big socialiser, and was bountiful in company. He also changed blondes fairly regularly. His first boat was a Bayliner, a petrol-engined American sports cruiser, which he asked me to collect from Shamrock Quay, Southampton and deliver to Hull. After loading, departure was delayed due to the late transfer of funds and incorrect paperwork. Frantic phone calls to David and his PA eventually brought about the release of the boat and I was able to proceed. Arriving at Hull Marina early on yet another eventful Friday afternoon to launch this craft, scornfully referred to by proper sailors as a "Tupperware Box" or even "Binliner", David became the victim of maritime snobbery.

The marina manager at the time was a sailing enthusiast whose ambition was to run a south coast marina. This ambition, which was ultimately fulfilled, meant that as we arrived he was in the process of grovelling to a "Round the World" yachtie team whose boat had suffered a damaged keel. The yacht was suspended in the hoist slings and all other matters were put on hold whilst repairs were completed.

"Have a beer," David said as we sat on the back of the trailer, "your part in this whole bloody operation is the only bit that's gone right."

The marina manager appeared and said to David somewhat disdainfully and completely dismissively;

"Awfully sorry old boy but we've got 'Crigthton's Naturally' in the hoist and she's having her keel attended to, so we won't be able to launch you until Monday."

His look of contempt began to change as David slowly rocked to his feet. David was as wide as he was tall and he took the manager by the lapels of his jacket and leaned him over the edge of the quay.

"Look pal, if my boat doesn't go into the water *this* afternoon, you ******* will."

With a face now pale and ashen and with a voice now trembling somewhat, the arrogance gave way to subservience.

"I'll see what can be done." And guess what, within half an hour, David's boat was launched. David became the 'life and soul' or 'scourge' of the marina depending on how you judge his behaviour. He would have boozy nights round the pubs of Hull and bring a crowd back to his boat for a party. The Bayliner became too cramped for his social scene and we were hired to collect a Sea Ray 36 from Prossers Marine at Renfrew. He specified that the boat had to be shrink wrapped for travel and in our naivety Max and I took about ten rolls of cellophane from the yard normally used to shrink wrap palletized products. With extreme and time consuming difficulty, we managed to wrap the whole boat by going up, over, across, down, underneath, up, over, across, down, underneath about fifty times, overlapping the previous layer to complete the coverage. It looked neat and would protect 'Weeladeela' from the road dirt, grit and spray for the journey back to Hull, keeping the showroom shine which Prossers had prepared. By the time we stopped to check the load at Bothwell Services just south of Glasgow the last shreds of the shrink wrap were clinging to the places where the straps restrained the boat. To be honest boat shrink wrapping involves proper equipment, heat sealing and a cost of up to a thousand pounds.

We were lucky, the elements were kind to us and the boat arrived in Hull more or less as it had left Renfrew, apart from some small scraps of cellophane hiding in some nooks and crannies. This petrol engine sports cruiser gave David a much enhanced social status and the parties became bigger and louder.

The Sea Ray was an expensive beast to run, burning around five hundred pounds in petrol to go to Spurn Point and back when petrol was still under fifty pence a litre!

David could behave very aggressively without much provocation. One Saturday night on his way to Hull he was stopped in his Range Rover, breathalysed and locked up in Goole Police Station. Refusing to share a cell with drunken youths from the town, he wrecked the police cell.

He told me later, "Dougy, it was like something from a western; I smashed every piece of furniture like it was polystyrene!" His subsequent conviction for criminal damage, common assault and drunk driving resulted among other things, in the loss of his driving licence. From then on his lawyer became his chauffeur!

Fisherman's Friend

One day when cruising on the River Ouse near York he antagonized or was antagonised by, some fishermen who shouted at him for speeding. There is a speed limit on the river and there are often altercations between anglers and boaters. He turned "Weeladeela" round, gave it full throttle on both engines and charged past the line of fishermen on the riverbank. The bow wave hit the shore; first of all washing the anglers up the bank with their tackle spread asunder, and then drenching them again as the water flowed back to the channel. David turned again and slowly cruised back to the saturated fishermen.

"Gentlemen, now that was speeding."

A larger than life character, now sadly deceased.

"I've heard you'll have a go," said a gruff voice on the telephone. "How much to take my boat from Dewsbury to Hull?"

"What is it, yacht or cruiser?" I replied, reaching for the quote book to enter the details.

"Steel cruiser, built it myself. I'm Peter Marshal Fire Escapes," he volunteered, as if that would mean anything to me.

"Length?"

"About forty two foot"

"Beam?"

"About thirteen six"

"Height?"

"About fourteen six at the moment"

"Weight?"

"About nine tons at the moment"

The words 'about' and 'at the moment' and the broad Yorkshire accent suggested that the job just might not be straightforward. Not that the broad Yorkshire accent would imply any dishonesty or bad practice, more a matter of fact kind of confidence that whatever has to be done, can be done and therefore *will* be done. Confirmation followed.

"It's my factory but I've sold it t' workforce. They reckon as they can do t'job better and they want me and me boat aht. Boat's in a corner where there are no doors, the street outside is only thirty foot wide . . . and I've 'eard you'll 'ave a go!"

A compliment indeed and we were developing a reputation for doing some awkward jobs so this was worth looking at.

"Normally this journey would be priced as a day rate but I think a site visit would be worthwhile," I said, realising that 'ave a go' meant that nothing would be as it was described and that some planning would be necessary. A visit for the next day was agreed and I was given a tour of the factory and an appraisal of the new management before reaching the boat.

"Never would allow that when t'factory were mine," said Peter, referring to a radio blasting pop music on the workshop floor. "I'd 'ave put an 'ammer through it, you can't work properly wi' all that noise!"

Actually, Peter was deaf, so I wondered why the radio bothered him. Perhaps it was the new regime, which worked in a less strict atmosphere than when he was in charge that was the real source of the annoyance. Anyway, he coped by lip-reading. We walked through the dusty factory. The building was originally a mill in typical West Yorkshire tradition, built of gritstone blocks on a narrow ledge of land near the river. The ex-employees, now labouring for themselves, worked on as we surveyed the boat. Measurements were confirmed but height was a problem; only five inches gap between the flybridge throttle controls and the factory roof, and the keel was on the floor save for thin plywood packers! But worse, there was no door in the gritstone walls anywhere near the boat.

"Don't worry about that, I've got some machinery removal specialists organised to get it out. All the stone blocks will be numbered so we'll just knock the wall down, slide the boat out and rebuild the wall! Outside the factory a short pavement fell to a cobbled street. At the other side of the street a wall about fifteen feet high protected a yard at the back of some terraced houses. The boat was longer than the width of the street. Peter was equally dismissive of this becoming any kind of a problem.

"If we can't turn t'boat before it's out of t' factory we'll have to knock t' other wall down."

Sunday morning, Police advised of route, road closure arranged, we arrived to find a scene reminiscent of a scene from "The Last of The Summer Wine".

The stone blocks had been numbered, extracted and put aside ready for replacement but had been stolen. A team of lads had been despatched to have a word with the known culprits and the blocks had been returned. A small crowd had gathered nearby and an enterprising local was taking bets on the chances of success of the job. Peter's wife brought bacon butties for the crew of helpers then

I've 'eard you'll 'ave a go!

retreated home to tend the garden. Crisps and soft drinks were being dispensed to onlookers at the end of the street as the windows of nearby houses filled with anxious faces, all wondering how the boat could be removed.

The boat was jacked onto small steel rollers and a lorry mounted crane with a retracting arm was used to pull it inch by inch out of the factory. Another crane was sited near the 'hole in the wall' to pick up the boat when it emerged. Men were stationed on the deck to check for clearance at every stage. The gaps above and at either side were minimal. The throttle controls scraped a steel roof beam but squeezed past. Carpets were hung along the sides of the boat to prevent scratching. Slowly the craft was winched into the daylight, the gleaming white hull contrasting with the surrounding stone and cobbles. Just as the rollers came to the edge of the pavement, the limit to which the boat could be pulled, the team attached a strap from the crane to take the weight of the front of the boat.

With the front of the boat airborne and the aft part still buried in the factory the slow emergence continued.

The prow was now close to the wall at the opposite side of the street. Fingers were crossed and breath was held. The next few moments would be crucial. A second strap was attached to the stern of the boat, which now straddled the street as the crane took the full weight.

"How many?" I mouthed to the crane driver, asking for clarification of the weight. He opened his hand once, twice, three times, then presented two fingers.

"Seventeen Tons! Never!" said I. The crane driver nodded vigorously looking rather anxious that he might not be able to cope with the weight. Perhaps he had set up the crane on the assumption that the words 'about nine tons at the moment' bore some relevance to reality.

"Peter, the crane driver says it weighs seventeen tons, you said about nine!"

"Ah well, t' plans said four mill' but I made it out o' six mill' just to be on t' safe side," Peter replied with a smile and a shrug.

The boat was turned, successfully missing the walls on either side of the road but unfortunately the wrong way round for loading onto the trailer. After negotiating the overgrown factory yard and a track along the riverbank I could reverse under the crane facing in the right direction. The boat was lowered onto the trailer much to the relief of all the assembled company. A cheer went up as the crane let go of the craft.

The rest of the day was almost an anti-climax. A short run through narrow streets led to the M62 and proceeding slowly with the extra weight, two hours later we were in Hull. Whilst entering the marina compound the trailer suffered a puncture, a small setback after such an unusual enterprise.

A common practice in boatbuilding is for one firm to

build the hull and superstructure out of GRP, fibreglass to you and me, and leave the fitting out to others, sometimes even the owners. A shopkeeper in a South Yorkshire town initially bought one Aquabell hull from the builders on the Norfolk Broads and fitted it out behind a garage near one of his shops. I went to collect the moulding and parked outside the Aquafibre factory at Rackheath one dark Sunday night. It was pitch black outside and luckily I had been pre-warned about the fearsome guard dog. Any movement outside the vehicle, such as checking the tyres would unleash a blood curdling noise, which would carry on for about a minute. Thankfully it was a mechanical guard dog, triggered by any activity outside the shed. After a somewhat disturbed night, when everything from a hedgehog to an owl set the wretched hound off in a fit, I awoke to load the hull.

There are lessons to be learnt here; boat mouldings behave like a tube of toothpaste when trying to strap them to the trailer. First, there are no lashing points so long straps must be used going right over the whole boat giving increased risk of slipping, vibrating and chafing the polished gel coat. Second, tighten one strap that looks to be slack and the hull changes shape and slackens the next strap! Anyway, the hull was delivered to Barry near his home and he completed a superb fit-out in a very short time. So off I go to Whitby where, whilst waiting to unload it, Barry sells it 'off the back of the lorry'. So Barry buys another moulding, I collect it from Rackheath - beware of the mechanical dog once again - deliver it to South Yorkshire, Barry fits it out and I go to collect it to take to Whitby. This one is launched and off I go again!

Barry built up such a fine reputation for the quality of his fitting out that he could guarantee to sell any boat even before it was launched. One delivery to Whitby was complimented by a reload of an earlier fit-out that had been sold to a fisherman in Orkney, which meant another trip to

Splash 'N' Cash

Scotland for me, meeting the buyer at Wick and indulging in a celebration of local produce, reluctantly of course but a necessary part of customer relations. Barry stepped up production and at one point had two moulds behind the garage in his home town being fitted out.

Barry's original intention had been to build himself a fishing boat to take fishing parties out from Whitby but every time a completed Aquabell was delivered, someone would bid for it and Barry would go and build another. Eventually he managed to keep one for his own use and the fishing party project got under way with regular trips for sea anglers. In the meantime, however, there was another development. Meant partly as a joke, partly admiration but definitely not for advertising purposes for advertising was not necessary, Barry's daughter made out a Business Card using one of those DIY printing machines. The cards proclaimed Barry's prowess as a 'Master Boatbuilder'. Unfortunately, one of the cards fell into the hands of the Inland Revenue, resulting in intensive enquiries and eventually the loss of at least one of his shops.

In the early days of boat haulage I often had to refer to Mad Max to ascertain the nature of a particular boat, it's keel configuration and general suitability for being 'roaded'. Even now, after over twenty years of experience there are new things to learn, different shapes to accommodate and it's still worth seeking advice. Max assured me that we could load a Grand Banks 42 Trawler Yacht but it would be necessary to remove the flybridge. The customer accepted this but in retrospect I think he wished he had asked around for more options. In the event, Max and I went to Inverkip, yes, another trip to Scotland, loaded the boat mid-morning, then set about removing the flybridge. We had obtained diagrams of the hydraulics and the wiring which Max soon disconnected. I set about trying to undo the body of the flybridge, which had been screwed to the deck, then covered with a skin of fibreglass. Every screw had to be located, the fibreglass ground out from over the screw head and then the screw extracted. I gave up counting after removing over seven hundred! By dusk we were ready to relocate the body onto the foredeck and secure it. One of the marina staff stayed behind to make the transfer with the crane. It was now nearly dark but we were almost ready to move. I phoned Strathclyde Police and quoted our incident number, issued when an escort is required, and said we would be ready at first light to be escorted out of the area. We were passed from department to department, no one seeming to want to get involved with us. Finally, we got an ultimatum. Mrs. Windsor, her Majesty even, was due to visit Greenock the following day and all abnormal load movements and escorts were postponed until the day after. After some fourteen hours preparing to load the boat safely, we were thwarted by the Royal Family taking precedence!

We showered and crossed the road into Inverkip village to seek food and refreshment. Things have improved somewhat in the intervening years but at that time you could get a drink in Scotland but very little to eat after about seven-thirty in the evening. As there was no food available in this village we downed a swift pint of 'Twenty Shilling' or whatever value was the title of the beer at the time, chased it down with a malt and took a taxi to Wemyss Bay. Apart from an oil-fired Power Station, built when that fuel was cheap, whose chimney is a landmark for motorists and mariners alike and a ferry to the beautiful Isle of Bute, there is little of note at Wemyss. But there was a Chinese restaurant. Max and I ate well and drank more whisky, expecting to be stuck at Inverkip for over twenty-four hours. We took a taxi back to the marina.

At half past midnight the phone rang.

"Good morning, it's Sergeant Patterson, Strathclyde Police. Our boys will come and get you away before the royal visit. Be ready at O Four Thirty!"

Sharp intake of breath and huge intake of water! I drank about a gallon of water, desperate to dilute the effects of the whisky. I ordered Max to do the same but he just crashed out in the stern cabin of the boat. I sat in the drivers' seat for what remained of the night, not daring to sleep in case I was still comatose when the police arrived. They came, right on time. I filled my mouth with mints and tried to avoid close contact.

"Where's your attendant?"

"Oh, he's still in bed. I'll get him up."

Max must have been having a bad dream. He went berserk when awoken, shouting expletives to, and about the police. I think he believed he'd been shipwrecked or boarded by pirates, such was the noise and pandemonium. Fortunately, as he was still inside the boat, the noise did not carry clearly. When he appeared, obviously the worse for wear I pushed him into the lorry despite his abusive protestations and we set off!

Approaching a low bridge in Gourock the police

Max meets his match!

stopped us to check that we were aware of the height of the load. This gave them a chance to look round the load and pointed out that a marker light attached to a retaining strap on the off side was not working. Whilst not a legal requirement and there just to highlight the extremity of the load, they insisted, "If it's there it must be lit."

I was using Paul's unit as he was on holiday, and I couldn't find his stash of spare bulbs. The police were now tapping their fingers on the roof of their car, showing increasing impatience and looking ready to park us up and leave us there. That's not as unlikely as it may seem, I assure you. I took a bulb from the nearside of the trailer and hoped that the swap would not be seen from the patrol car. We set off again and got through Glasgow without further incident. When the police left us we pulled into a service area and caught up with some much needed sleep. After a while, alcohol level hopefully down below the legal limit, we proceeded to Hartlepool. The Queen never bothered to apologise for causing such disruption but the incident is one of many to show the Scottish Police in a good light. Strathclyde in particular will often make an extra effort to help with abnormal loads.

There is a saying, "Age doesn't come alone," and I must reflect on a couple of embarrassing mistakes, one at my expense, one caused by a customer, both due to mishearing words of a crucial nature. I'm going deaf and the caller had a stammer, resulting in a conversation something like this.

"Ow Ow Ow Mu-Mu Much to t-t-take m-m my M-m m motor c-c c cruiser f-f from B-B B Beverley t-t to B-B B Bridlington?

"Well that depends...' I start to reply but the caller interrupts...

"a-a and b b back again in a-a f-f f ortnight?"

Not a likely job I thought but perhaps there was a regatta and the customer was just going for that or something similar. It's not unheard of.

"How big is it and what does it weigh?" was my reply.

"Ooh Ooh, it it it's ever so he-he heavy," the caller replied.

"We'll have to hire a crane or load it at the Beck where Steve has a crane," I continued, trying to put the whole project into a nutshell to save stuttering time.

"I-I I Ire a crane?" said my potential customer, sounding rather anxious.

"Yes," I said, "We can't self load."

"Ooh Ooh No," the voice changed from anxious to desperate. I began to wonder if I had heard him correctly.

"You did say motor cruiser, did you not?"

"No No No No... M-M M Motorbility Scooter!"
Oops!

Not my fault that time but an embarrassing moment,

Deaf and daft

nay, International Incident occurred when I delivered a Corvette cruiser to Dover Marina. The owner asked for help to put it on its mooring when launched and I duly obliged, at least I held the rope and jumped ashore to secure it. As we walked back across the car park a car with a foreign registration, which for the purpose of the story was German but could perhaps have been French or Belgian approached, apparently to ask directions. No, on second thoughts the driver was formal and polite so must have been German. He stopped near my customer, a local man, and as such would know the directions, if that was to be the enquiry. Indeed it was.

"Scuz me Zur, could you pliz tell me ze way to ze Spidd Firr?"

I know what I thought he had said but left it to the local man to reply and point him in the right direction.

"Turn around, go back to that roundabout, go up the hill, turn right at the next roundabout following the brown sign, turn left and you're there."

The driver looked puzzled.

"I donnt zink zo Zur."

"Listen, now I live round here and I'm telling you; turn around go back to that roundabout , go up the hill, turn right at the next roundabout following the brown sign, turn next left and you're there!" repeated our local boy with considerable vehemence.

"Oh, OK Zur, Zank You Zur" and he did as he had been told. I turned round to see the huge sign 'Speed Ferry' and pointed it out to my customer.

"Oh Bloody Hell, I thought he said Spitfire, so I've sent him to the Battle Of Britain Museum!"

"It takes all sorts to make a world," so the saying goes and boating certainly has 'all sorts' of people, perhaps reflecting society but maybe including a high proportion of eccentrics and 'characters'. First impressions are important but my judgements are not always right first time but at least with a phone conversation one can get an inkling as to the nature of the individual. Not so with the impersonal modern medium, the e-mail or worse, the text. One phone call to request a quote to move a cruiser from Goole to a marina over the other side of the Pennines left me feeling curious about the owner.

The boat was a "Cleopatra 27" which with hindsight could have been a cryptic clue. In a deep brown voice the caller asked for price and availability for the move but when the name given was 'Shelley' I thought I had misheard it. Subsequent conversations were equally confusing and the baritone voiced "Shelley" had a partner called Jane. Shelley assured me that Jane would pay me at the point of delivery. I duly collected the boat and crossed the Pennines into the Red Rose County arriving at the destination around lunchtime. 'Shelley' was 'nine out of ten' for the famous Lily Savage or perhaps a fan of the Egyptian femme fatal; bouffant hair-do, long straight

Queen Of The Waves

evening gown with three quarter sleeves and slit all the way up to the crutch, made up and dressed up to the nines! She (he) hitched up the long dress, clambered aboard the boat and helped prepare it for craning. Against all the rules she (he) remained aboard as the boat was hoisted upwards and over the quayside. Straightening the dress she (he) posed for the onlookers holding one of the crane straps with one hand and waving majestically with the other. Upon entering the water, she(he) started the boat and drove away to her (his) mooring. I was approached by a lady bearing cash. She (he no she) introduced herself as Jane and paid me for the delivery. The crane driver, with typical scouse humour came over and summed them up;

"They're all right yer know, those two, but yer know what they are dontcha, they're transformers."

A couple of weeks later I was in the same marina and saw 'Shelley' again, still frocked and bouffan'd up. It was a hot day and as she (he) was sawing something on top of

Never mind the crew, save the dog for goodness sake!

a steel barrel. Suddenly, cursing with that familiar baritone voice, "It's bloody hot", off came the big wig to reveal a highly polished bald head!

Transferring our skills from road to water is not always advisable as Paul and his son Alex discovered when collecting a Moonraker from Bristol Marina. The owner, new to boating having just purchased the craft, asked them to help collect the boat from its mooring and bring it to the hoisting area. He admitted to a lack of familiarity with the boat so Paul and Alex agreed to help with the ropes and fenders. Settling down at the helm, roll-up between lips, the picture of a cool pilot, the owner pulled the throttles firmly, the boat shot ahead, then full astern, hard to port, hard to starboard, collided with a yacht, a cruiser and the fuel pontoon, then careered out of the marina into the river.

Meanwhile a loopy dog, sensing danger is trying to jump off. Cruising trip boats with customers enjoying afternoon tea are treated to a demonstration of how not to drive a motor boat, feel no concern for our reluctant crew but gasp with horror as the dog tries a reverse twist, somersault and double pike from the flybridge. Paul and Alex can both cope with danger and excitement but this was altogether too much. They hung on to the guard-rail for dear life!

CHAPTER NINE
Gardens, Fields & Driveways

The optimism of boat owners knows no limits. Although we haven't kept accurate records I would be fairly sure that we have obliged one of these requests well over a hundred times.

"I'm going to put her next to my house, spend six months restoring her, then you can come back and take her to the marina."

Or; "My mate has a bit of land where I can put the boat and do it up."

Or; "There's a field at the end of our road and I can put my boat there until the farmer wants to sow seeds in the Spring. I'll have it ready to launch by then."

Or; "It's going down a track to a big yard. There's loads of room, they get trucks in there all the time."

Of those which we have installed in these obscure locations, we have been back to collect maybe ten of them. 'Number One' for the sheer time involved is a steel yacht bought brand new as a shell for a fitting out programme, which the owner anticipated would take a maximum of two years. It was squeezed between the owner's house and the neighbour's cottage in a village adjacent to the A63 in East Yorkshire. That was in 1989 and it's still there! Occasionally I see the owner who is a Humber Pilot and he always says, "Soon be ready."

'Kalamunda' was a 'home finish' job that we had the pleasure of collecting as the haulier who delivered the shell some years previously had retired. It was behind some

Soon be Ready?

cottages at an East Yorkshire village in the Holderness area, east of Hull. The journey to Hull Marina required a diversion through Hull Docks to avoid a low bridge. It was a rare pleasure to get in and out of Hull docks in a matter of minutes and without delay and without abuse from the dockers.

A steel cruiser, a Bruce Roberts TCF40 to be pedantic, built in a barn near York, caused a near disaster with the health and safety brigade. The boat was on a yard trailer (steel frame and solid wheels) and I could not get Dobbin onto the site. A tractor was used to drag the boat to the nearest road which happened to be adjacent to the newly electrified East Coast Railway line. We blocked the road with our vehicles; the tractor and trailer, Dobbin and trailer and the crane. Trains passed by, some hooting as they passed. Some people waved from the carriages. We felt like we were in a scene from The Railway Children. It must have looked unusual from the train to see a boat hanging in the air on the end of a crane, miles from the nearest water. A small queue of vehicles built up in both directions and most drivers waited patiently as the boat was slowly transferred from the yard trailer to the care and protection of Dobbin. Just as the boat was more or less settled and chocked safely, a team from British Rail came charging along the embankment passing the row of cars on the road.

"Hold it right there. You cannot lift that boat with the crane so near to the power lines. You will have to take the boat away on that trailer. If you try to use that crane we shall have to cut the power to the railway and that will cost you thousands!"

It seemed they thought the operation was about to take place, in other words the reverse of what had actually just happened. Men in orange coats took up positions to prevent the boat being lifted. Reluctantly, we submitted to their demands, the tractor and trailer returned to the farm and Dobbin, John the boat owner and I set off for Poole. Job done! In the cabin John had left a kettle, full of water on top of a portable gas stove. It was still there at Poole, without a drop spilt. Careful driving or what? For reasons of domestic disharmony we brought the boat back two weeks later but into the river at Naburn, not by the railway line!

A sequel to that event happened many years later when Paul was delivering a large Haines cruiser to a Fenland waterway. There were limited craning positions but the boat was successfully lifted off and into the water. The cavalry arrived in the guise of the men from the Environment Agency and took command of the scene.

"Nobody move. Cranes must not be used here!" shouted the EA jobsworth. Paul kept his head down and tidied up the trailer ready to leave. Likewise, the crane driver turned his back and de-rigged his crane ready to move off site. Meanwhile the boat owner checked his boat, started up and prepared to motor away to his

No Cranes Allowed

mooring. Suddenly it dawned on Jobsworth that the crime was not about to take place but had already been committed. So he set off to apprehend the crane driver but he was already on the move. He turned to catch Paul but was again too late. So jobsworth had to catch the boat owner but he'd slipped his mooring and was on his way down the channel! Stable door and bolting horses come to mind for these two incidents.

There was a large steel yacht built by the canal in Wakefield. There had been so many attempts to move it that the West Yorkshire police organised the removal of the street furniture to permit transit to the M62. We priced up for transport for at least two different owners on different occasions but were always thwarted by various circumstances. It is a feature of boating that there always seems to be another optimist to take on a lost cause for removal and renovation. This vessel, however, was cast off and let slip into the canal basin where it sank, some wag having painted 'Titanic' on the stern that was left protruding out of the water.

Another steel boat, a long keel yacht and much smaller, had been built nearby. It was unusual in that it appeared to stand up on its own but closer inspection showed it welded to a girder extending out from an adjacent engineering works. We had to organise a road closure, employ a welder to burn off the join and hire a crane to lift the boat over the factory. Unfortunately, the extension of the girder in the factory supported not only the structure of the building but also was attached to several items of machinery. The boat had been a counterbalance to all this mass and the cutting of the join destabilised the whole building. Inside the factory was apparently a scene of chaos. I took the boat to a site in Kent near to the construction site for the Channel Tunnel, where the owner arrived to see the rusty hulk off-loaded.

"Isn't she a beauty!" he exclaimed, going into rapturous praise for the prowess of that type of hull in the waters around Kent. Not for the last time did a true sailor seem more than a little deranged. To me, a mere land-lubber, the hulk seemed destined never to float (by that I mean the boat not the owner).

A dedicated mariner and skilled DIY boat-builder, fitted out an Atlantic 38 motor cruiser in the garden of his house at Penistone, between Sheffield and Manchester. Like Peter Marshall fire escapes, Brian had a positive attitude; if it has to be done this way or that way, it shall be done and that's the end of it.

The boat weighing around nine tons had to be lifted over four houses. A thousand ton crane was employed to lift the vessel. Four truck loads of sand were dumped under the corners of the crane to spread the weight of the legs. Power lines had to be switched off, a house evacuated, a road closure arranged and a very low bridge to be squeezed under just to make things interesting. Some technicality had not been followed but a considerate policeman allowed the load to proceed and the boat safely reached Hull. We must have done the job OK because we have subsequently moved 'C-Life' from Plymouth to Newark, and then from Southsea to Lincoln.

Ebay, the modern means of buying and selling has exposed a number of boats in obscure locations and the blinkered optimism of the buyers who seem to buy first then suffer the consequences. The first ebay deal that came our way was from a lady who had bought a lifeboat at a place in Somerset and asked me for a quote to take it to Essex. After gleaning that it was a ship's lifeboat, not a RNLI type, I was puzzled by the location. It turned out to have been placed behind a house in a village, nowhere near any water. The subsequent years had not been kind to the craft as the village had enjoyed boom time popularity and new house building had stranded the boat out of reach of car drivers, never mind boat transporters. Absolutely no chance!

The next ebay deal was another situation where the 'Buyer Beware' rule was ignored. In a field near Crawley in Sussex there was, and probably still is, a thirty-eight foot, long-keeled yacht. It was placed there many years ago and was advertised and sold on ebay as an 'on-going project'. The lucky purchaser discovered that the field was receiving EU grants for 'Set Aside'. The crafty owner of the farm had decreed that the purchaser would have to pay rent until the boat was removed but there would be no access on his land because 'Set Aside' payments dictate that no vehicles cross the designated area. So, the crane would have to be set up in the adjacent field. This field was not on 'set aside', nor did it grow crops, nor did it graze animals; it housed the landing lights for Gatwick Airport. Imagine the likelihood of getting permission to operate a crane near the flight path? I don't think so!

One moderately successful ebay deal did occur,

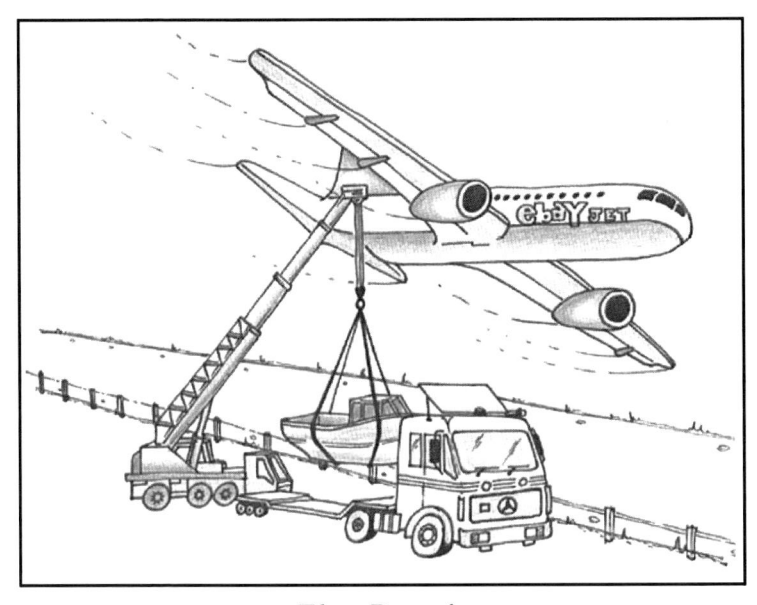

Ebay Bargain

although not without drama. A mining engineer spent some of the last years of his working life building a cruiser on a disused mine site near Leicester. He had retired to a place in Lincolnshire and found difficulty in getting to the site to work on his boat, so he asked us to take it to near Market Rasen, to a farm where he could get it into a barn. The disused mine had become overgrown with quite well established bushes and trees and the boat had to be moved on makeshift rollers to get into a space where a crane could operate. Eventually, it was loaded but the journey was delayed by the need to remove hardboard and chipboard panels that clad the boat. The journey to Market Rasen was fairly straightforward and the farming community provided improvised lifting gear to off-load the craft. So far, so good. Sadly the old miner had become an old timer and was unable to complete his project. He had managed some progress since the move and the boat was structurally sound so he took advice and put it on ebay. We must have had five or six enquiries from people who claimed to have won the bidding but the successful bidder lived near Inverness, providing yet another trip to Scotland. The farmers wouldn't improvise for the reload (maybe they didn't like Scotsmen), so a proper crane had to be hired. So much for ebay deals.

Farmers' fields have become the repository for many boats over the years and where the land is not worked, weeds grow. Weeds give way to bushes, bushes to trees. And so to a meadow near Tydesley, near Wigan, where a Bruce Roberts yacht - She's a classic you know! - had been festering for over twenty years. The shell had been put into the field in 1974 and after some early effort the owner gave up. By the time I went to relocate it in 1999 the meadow had become a forest. The owners asked for a Saturday collection as the road was single track and there would be less traffic. There were plenty of helpers, which was fortunate because the jungle had to be cleared before the crane and the truck could get near the boat. It took well into the afternoon before we could reverse off the road and get set up. After all this forestry work, loading was almost an anticlimax, and was speedily completed. A bonus was the absence of all the usual claptrap which complicates yacht movements; no mast, no boom, no sails, no loose items at all, so we were soon strapped down and ready to struggle out of the jungle. After a few yards on tarmac I pulled up to check the condition of the lorry, trailer and of course the security of the boat. This is normal practice but made more imperative due to the rough ride through the jungle. To my surprise and concern the two owners came up and started beating the sides of the boat with heavy sticks.

Must be some sort of yachtie ritual, I thought, they're maybe driving away evil spirits or some mariners' superstition. Normally to ask would invite trouble as it would be assumed that you knew the rules about

Unwanted Guests

albatrosses, name changes and other odd features of sailors' behaviour but beating the boat with sticks? Maybe it's like the saying, "A Woman, a dog and a walnut tree, the more you beat them the better they be".

Perhaps boats too. So I asked the question.

"There are two enormous wasp nests in there and we're trying to dislodge them!"

Load briefly checked, I was back in the cab double quick, windows shut and away! I do believe I saw a plume of the angry beasties streaming out from the top of the boat as I climbed Windy Ridge on the M62. The boat, minus its tiny livestock was safely delivered.

How it arrived there I have no idea but a Birchwood cruiser was to be collected from the Highway Vehicle Recovery depot on the A1 south of Ferrybridge and delivered to Naburn. The A1 at that point was dual carriageway but the depot was badly sited for south bound traffic due to a crown in the road. It was necessary to reverse out, reverse up the short 'In' slip, then accelerate

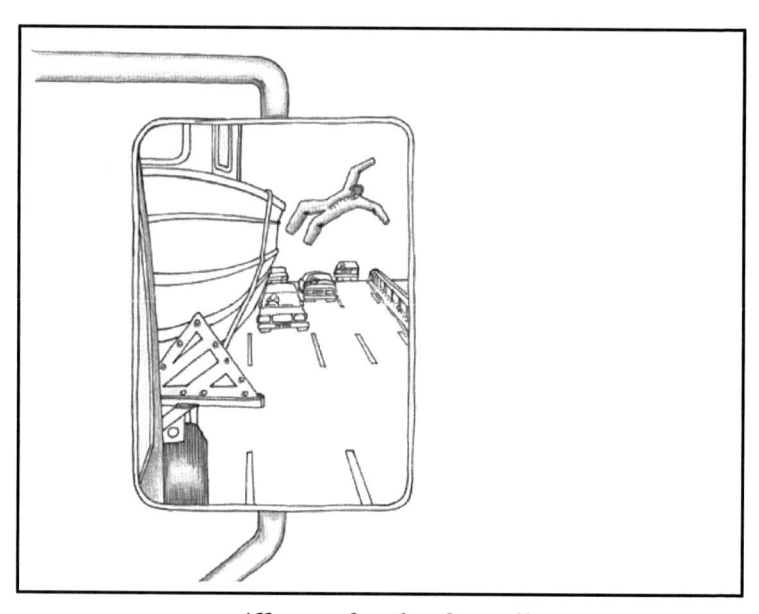

__All over for the Overall__

quickly forward using both the 'In' slip and 'Out' slip and hopefully enter the first lane at a speed merging with the traffic. Brave men, some without 'hi-viz' jackets would you believe, stood on the verge and tried to slow the main road traffic by waving frantically at the oncoming vehicles. Little Mandy was never very athletic and we felt particularly vulnerable as we joined the madding throng of trucks, cars and buses. Half expecting collision, screeching brakes or at least angry hornblowing, I was suddenly distracted by a figure lurching upwards, visible in a flash in the off-side mirror. In my state of nervous apprehension for a split second it looked like one of the workmen hurled into the air by impact against the boat. A second glance brought welcome relief. It was my boiler suit, left on the battery box, caught up by the wind, unfurled and thrown high into the air. I did not go back to retrieve it.

CHAPTER TEN
Knock, Knock, Knockin' On Dobbin's Door

Being away from home all week is a mixed blessing, no more mixed than when sharing primitive facilities with another person. Despite the comforts of modern sleeper cabs it is still a strange way of life, made even more difficult by the abhorrence shown by the public to the drivers who deliver every item that gets into the shops. Local authorities have certain social responsibilities, many backed by law. They must look after themselves of course and indeed many of our wealthiest citizens are council employees receiving huge salaries on the self-promoted notion that they could earn more in commerce or industry so have to be paid vast sums to keep them in 'public service'. A dubious equation for sure. They must also provide education, social housing, grass cutting, street lighting, road sweeping, refuse collection etcetera, etcetera, but not it seems reasonable parking facilities for lorries. So drivers park where they can, sometimes where they shouldn't and often without access to toilets, showers, food or refreshment.

The law rightly insists that drivers get proper rest in the interest of road safety. The long, lonely hours incarcerated in the vehicle lead to dreaming and fantasizing and in some locations the fantasies become reality with visits from the 'ladies of the night'. Our privileged situation in being able to park overnight in marinas and boatyards leads to a better class of fantasy altogether. Our opulent surroundings and well equipped vehicles attract the attention of celebrity ladies, sort of

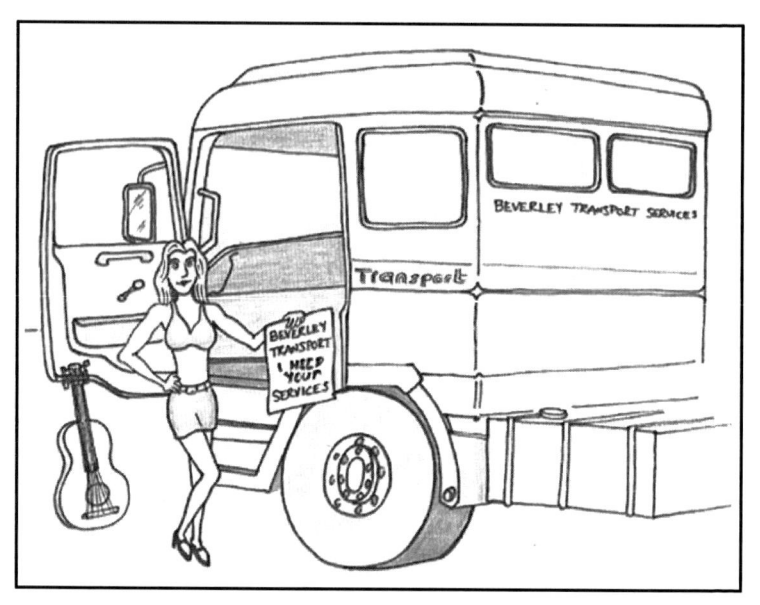

May I Ride in Your Lorry?

'Boat Mover's Groupies'. Over the years we have had to keep the doors locked to rebuff the determined advances of Julie Christie, Susan George, Shania Twain, Sheryl Crow, Cameron Diaz and even those girls from the Corrs (leave your brother out of it please) and many more.

    Such is the perceived luxury of sleeping in the cab that the Inland Revenue and HM Customs give serious attention to this 'perk' of the job. Over the years as the authorities have grudgingly given a small tax free allowance for drivers using sleeper cabs, they have sought perniciously to prove abuse of the allowance and snatch it back. It is true that some employers may offer drivers a payment of a 'Night Out' when actually parked back at base but if the drivers are away all week the payment is fully justified. Once, when being interrogated by a VAT inspector on how we checked validity when making Subsistence payments, how did I know they were away? did I insist on receipts for food purchased? and other nonsensical questions, I asked how he was treated if ever

VATman's new accommodation

he worked away from his base? He replied that he would be given vouchers for approved lodgings or booked into a hotel.

"What if your employer asked you to fit a tin box on top of your car and crawl into it to sleep?" I asked.

"I think we'll move on," he quietly responded, seeing no purpose in further interrogation.

One of his colleagues, a very determined female inspector with forensic skills, on another occasion, asked how much we paid and how we ask the drivers to prove that they needed a night out. Naturally, I declared that as I was running the operation I would be aware of anyone staying out unnecessarily and would know where the vehicles were during the night. Our intrepid inspector asked to see the payroll records and found that I had paid 'Q' for two nights out in one particular week.

"Where was he on those two nights," she demanded to know and I responded that I couldn't remember that far back.

"Well, you'll have the tachographs to jog your memory," she whined and demanded to see the charts.

"Look here, he parked at Newark and still had three hours driving time left on one of the days concerned. Why did he not get home? Newark is less than two hours away."

She knew how to 'read the cards' and not, I must add, for fortune telling, more fortune removing! I replied that he was either loading or unloading at Newark Marina or he would be using that place as a secure park, thereby helping with our insurance requirements. I felt it unwise to confess that his residence in Newark on the Tuesday would be for the purpose of attending the Bingo rather than for any business obligation. (We use several marinas for safe parking when en route between loading and unloading points and for this we are grateful to the marina operators. Also, apart from our creature comforts being seen to, it reassures the owners that we are not parking in dangerous locations with their boat)

"Well, you'll have to show me invoices that prove he was en route, starting a journey or ending a journey involving Newark."

Fortunately I could comply but it shows there is no hiding place for tax-free payments. For the attention of the tax authorities we have to keep tachographs for seven years. All this hassle for a few quid!

Over the years cabs have become more spacious with manufacturers competing to provide the most attractive surroundings with air conditioning, CD players, Bluetooth, blue movies, fridges and even microwaves now installed. When the width of the load exceeds eleven foot six inches, or three point five metres in new money, the vehicle must carry an Attendant or "Second Man". In a situation somewhat akin to the old "Red Flag" laws from the dawn of motoring the Attendant is there to warn other road users of the presence of the wide load. In our experience you can be equipped with luminous markers, flashing lights, beacons and be accompanied by a police escort and still be invisible to the average motorist! So the attendant's role is severely limited. Nevertheless, we always carry a 'Second Man' when required to do so. But finding someone suitable is not always easy. As it is in one sense a non-job, it is difficult to charge a reasonable amount to cover the costs of the attendant. On the other hand it cannot be expected that someone would fulfil this function for no reward. So it has often fallen to family, ex-colleagues, friends and friends of friends to be co-opted into this role. There is little to do apart from ride about, maybe help with loading, strapping down, stowing fenders or other simple tasks. We have even considered utilizing an inflatable doll to perform this function. (*Don't say it!*)

A traditional career structure for lorry drivers was for sons to ride with Dads, become driver's mates and then become drivers. This route to a lorry driving career has dried up with the ever more professional requirements for LGV attainment. Also, it has to be said that this industry is not very attractive from an economic or social point of view. So we have turned to the old school for our attendants. Neville, my father in law, enjoyed his boating trips observing the countryside from the lofty seating position.

"Ooh, can't you see a lot from up here" he exclaimed, an observation echoed by boat owners or boat owner's wives who were often thrust into the 'attendant ' position to help with the movement of their boat or simply to stay with their boat when it was being transported. Neville was a keen motorist in his own right but enjoyed the enhanced views from the lorry. He was also ex-RAF and would suddenly recognise an old airfield and add some history to the journey.

"That was the base for 625 squadron," or "that's

where the Dam Busters practiced." or "that's where they took off for the Norway campaign," or similar comments. His knowledge of the countryside of Britain was encyclopaedic. He was good company but as the years took their toll on his agility he was unable to continue. Paul would do an occasional trip when he could spare the time but was more interested in being on the other side of the lorry than in the passenger seat. His younger brother Iain would travel with Neil or me when on holiday from school or college. He was not really interested in transport but would fill the cab with books or magazines as he read his way round the country. He and I had a memorable trip to Lochgilphead - that's in Scotland don't you know? - to collect a burned out shell of a Colvic Watson yacht.

Pensioners are generally good at being 'second men'. They are usually of independent but modest means, they are free from day to day commitments, their wives encourage, even urge them to be away for as long as possible and they belong to a generation where reliability and punctuality can be taken as read. As long as facilities for bodily functions are sorted, there are few problems with pensioners.

John Hutchinson had worked for us as an agency driver on container work and had a mutual antipathy with Neil. They actually thought the world of each other but to hear the abuse they hurled at each other you'd think they were sworn enemies. John and Neil were a good team until John had to give up to care for his wife.

Rod Stoddard lived on his boat in Hull Marina and took over from 'Hutch' as "Second Man" and would regale us with amusing stories and anecdotes about his fellow berth-holders. He had a dry sense of humour. When the newly appointed manageress of the marina, apparently headhunted from a local theatre company, began the unwelcome changes that British Waterways inflicted on boat owners, Ron pointed out that they were prepared for a certain amount of drama but this was turning into a pantomime! Sadly, illness took its toll on poor Ron.

David Walker was almost hijacked into becoming a "Second man". He had held a variety of jobs during his working life and our paths first crossed when he was a boat salesman at York. He passed our name to many potential customers but he had a reputation for understating the dimensions of the craft in order to induce a lower price for transport.

(Another of our friends, Raymond Howe, also based near York has a good ready reckoner for boat owners and the size of their boats, hereafter to be known as 'Raymond's Rule; *"When they're in the pub, they're sixty foot long and twenty foot wide. When it comes to paying for anything, they're twenty foot long and six foot wide."*)

David Walker had sold a Nelson Forty Two to a lady in South Wales telling her it was ten-foot six wide. We priced up at this size but when Neil arrived to load it, it turned out to be twelve foot wide. David acted surprised but to cure him of his 'dimension blockage' Neil said "Right, you can be "Second man". To his credit David took a couple of days off and went away as the Attendant. It became an established question that whenever we got details of a potential boat movement from that source we would ask; "Is that the actual size or is it a Walkerism?" Since his retirement he has been an occasional "Second man" and has often helped us out of awkward situations at the last minute. His lovely wife Pam has now retired too so he has to ask permission to be allowed to travel.

Another David was recruited some years ago. He had previously worked for us both on HGV and PSV work. He had been in business and was planning to work abroad, developing WW1 battlefield tours.

A retired teacher, a retired truck salesman and several retired drivers have all been hijacked to ride round the country, share our facilities and indulge in deep and profound conversations.

We have always tried to be good employers and it seemed to me that the introduction of some young blood would be a good idea. The Victorians knew a thing or two about business so if they could employ young people to climb chimneys and sweep them surely we could employ young people for similar tasks on boats. They could climb up to the decks, remove canopies, stow fenders and other loose items and help secure the retaining straps. Perhaps we could make the job more fulfilling if we offered to train the attendant for other tasks or encourage them to have other jobs to fall back on when we didn't require their services. The trouble is whilst we the drivers love the job and consider it a privilege to move people's boats; it's not easy to impart this feeling on to others, especially to young people who probably have more lofty and more rewarding ambitions. It's also a lot to expect young people to break from their social scene and be away all week in what is perhaps a far from stimulating environment. Living and sleeping with us BOFs can't be much fun can it?

You have to sympathise with "second men" really, for their sleep would surely be something of a nightmare. Sharing with Neil would be spoiled by the snoring, wheezing and wailing, I would be up and down like the proverbial 'whores drawers' for a pee and Paul would be following the poor lad round with a duster and glass cleaner! But we've tried quite a few; one was very good but needed more money so moved on. One was quite good but slept most of the day and decided a college course held better prospects, several struggled to turn up and some just didn't seem interested in this activity despite the encouragement of parents or friends. When a person stops answering his phone, you know the cause is lost. So we resort to the old adage "Wear The Old Uns Out First".

"Rodders" is old school. As his voicemail message

> COULD YOU BE A
> **SECOND MAN?**
>
> Beverley Transport Services need **YOU**
>
> REQUIREMENTS:
> TURN UP.
> LIKE BEER.
> STAY AWAKE.
> TOLERATE DRIVERS.
> HELP LOAD AND UNLOAD.

'Second-Manning' Poster

says, "This is Rod, ex-pilot, two 'ology's..." and he lives on his boat. An exile from Yorkshire or doing missionary work in Norfolk however you care to look at it, Rodney has been a lifesaver for our 'Second man" requirements, helping out at very short notice when the youths described above have had better options. With investment in a Senior Citizens Railcard, Rod can make his way across England to join up with one or the other of our drivers. Initially unsure of his way about on the rail system he is now a walking timetable of routes and stations!

Steve Barden another resident of Brundall and a boat owner to boot, became a 'Second man" by default. When we substituted the original axles on Trailer One for those taken from Trailer Two, we also had the rear of the trailer 'beefed up' with some metalwork, removing the ramps and creating a protective space for the rear of the boats. Unfortunately, the fabrication was too low - will they ever listen - and with no time to get it altered I set off for Brundall. At the top of the hill, before dropping down to the station and the riverside boatyards, I stopped to adjust the trailer to reduce the risk of grounding. With the mudguards removed from the unit, the air could be dumped, lowering the front of the trailer and raising the back, thereby increasing ground clearance. The air bags in the trailer could also be inflated to raise the back even more. A chap walking his dog stopped to tell me, "The boatyards are down there," he said, pointing down Station Road. I explained that I knew and what I had been doing to avoid grounding the trailer. He took a small piece of ply wood from the well in the trailer, followed me down to the railway line and as the trailer began to scrape on the ground he slipped the plywood under the corner of the framework to let the trailer slide over the ground. Once safely over the lines I stopped to offer my thanks.

"I'll be in the bar with Rosie," he said and when I had parked up, I went to buy him a pint for his trouble. He proved to be an interesting character, retired from business in London, had a partner, "my Ee-layn" as he called her, and also had a boat and his dog Rosie. The corner by the bar, next to the payphone in The Yare was Steve Barden's place. A few weeks later, with the trailer modified to clear the road at Brundall railway crossing I was heading there again but needing a "second man". By ringing the pub and describing the character and his dog, I managed to talk to Steve and persuade him, and Rosie, to ride 'shotgun'. Both Neil and I had their good company on a number of occasions with Rosie riding on the engine cover. Steve told me of a project he and his "Ee-layn" were pursuing; the renovation of a house in a remote part of Spain. Elaine worked in London all week, stayed in their flat, had quite an important job in education, but they were going to marry when she took early retirement. There were many sessions in the corner of the Yare in the early evening when Steve walked Rosie and met up with early evening drinkers by the payphone. Sometimes boat owners would join in together with boat brokers like Jim Cole, James Frazer and Dan Money. It would be a rare night indeed when there was nobody we knew in the Yare. We would usually eat there too; no complaints but the same menu and the same 'specials' since before the millennium. Consistent and reliable at least.

In the summer of 2002 Angela and I drove to Spain to join up with Dai and Jenn, our lifelong friends. Holidays with Dai are like Field Study Courses, intensive lectures from himself and questions asked later. Sometimes we would be granted free time for a short period but not for long. On this occasion we were to study the hinterland of Havea, away from the overdeveloped coast. Dai and Jenn had been having trouble getting a faulty payment on a bank card recovered and suddenly, HSBC rang from England requiring that a document be faxed to help the process. So we went into Parcent, a little Spanish village. Dai and Jenn went to the bank to see if they had a fax machine while Angela and I walked around the dusty village square. It seemed the typical 'siesta time', nobody moving. Then I noticed a chap leave a bar wearing a cap to shield him from the sun, get into a small car and drive towards us. As it approached I saw British number plates and as it passed I saw a dog on the passenger seat, 'Rosie' and the driver was Steve Barden! I shouted and he accelerated away spewing dust into the air. Suddenly he stopped, looked in the mirror and waited as I walked up to his window. He thought he'd run over my foot, hence the hurried getaway. So at last we met his 'Ee-Layn', shared a coffee with them and marvelled at the artistic, innovative conversion of this corner house with spectacular views. What a coincidence! Sadly, Steve did no more "second manning", holding court in the Yare or getting full enjoyment out of the wonderful Spanish place. He passed away in 2004.

A modern term for the less able is someone with 'learning difficulties'. Is there an equivalent description for someone like me with 'ageing difficulties.'

We suffer 'failing faculties' etcetera, etcetera. So I am reduced to occasional trips out that don't fit for 'Q' and Paul, or when they are on holiday. Generally, it will be a long run, perhaps to Scotland, why not, and often overlapping a weekend. The staff and family think I am no longer capable of doing this alone so an old friend and colleague comes to do most of the driving. David Eling and I go back a long way and we have much in common. One of our agency customers operated livestock vehicles, collecting cattle from all over the UK. David was one of their drivers and had to suffer the indignity of having our drivers double-manning with him. To say the work was 'bent' would be an understatement. Hopefully by now an amnesty would release us from conviction. Cards (tachographs) were swapped to give the customer's drivers 'Nights Out'(tax free) instead of 'Nights In'(taxable). Routes were selected wherever possible to avoid weighbridges for obvious reasons. Often running in convoy the three cattle trucks were well known around the livestock markets of the UK. Trips to Anglesey for Irish cattle caused a number of incidents involving farmers, police and ministry men. Our man Andy, doubling up with Dave, aroused considerable suspicion concerning weight and hours regulations. The result was a 'Keystone Cops' scenario with a chase across the island, Andy dropped off to get the train home and Dave was stopped no less than six times between Holyhead and the M6. Dave reckons that five years of the cattle work was the equivalent of ten years as an 'ordinary' driver. He subsequently ran a commercial vehicle workshop and looked after the likes of Dobbin, Slug, two ERFs and our un-named Volvo. His business was taken over and he then ran a substantial bulk haulage operation for the buyout company. He is now a freelance driver and comes to us when required. Together we put the world to rights as we travel together. We shun the delights of the lorry cabs for proper accommodation in hotels, as befits gentlemen of our age and status. Sometimes the booking of these facilities is touch and go as we may not be sure where we may end up at the end of the day. But we have yet to be left stranded.

So we keep trying to find a young person who likes riding about the countryside, can get up early, help with loading and unloading, share a tin box with the driver, keep himself and his living area clean and present a friendly face to our customers.

CHAPTER ELEVEN
A Bad Dose Of Eczema

Dobbin had given many years of faithful service but was getting tired and his body was suffering from acute eczema.

Dobbin and I, then 'Q' and Dobbin visited many boatyards together, expanding the range of boats moved and making new friends for our business.

One day, on the A17 in Lincolnshire, Dobbin met a Volvo car, which was on the wrong side of the road. The Volvo, of course, had crumple zones and safety bars but Dobbin had none of these modern features. Dobbin took the impact bravely but was terminally damaged. Fortunately, Neil was not hurt. The body could take no more and crumbled like wholemeal biscuit. That's Dobbin's body, not Neil's. The years of faithful service came to a sad end and Dobbin was retired but his heart is probably still beating, powering a Chinese junk across Hong Kong harbour or similar situation.

Dobbin's figures make fascinating reading; Purchased for £3000. Operated for ten years. Costs apart from normal routine maintenance; 1 clutch, 2 prop shaft centre bearings, one compressor kit, one cylinder head gasket and a few electrical items. Sold back to dealer for £2000. Plus, write-off by insurers, £2000.

What a bargain Dobbin had been!

These figures demonstrate our belief that it doesn't really matter what is the age or make of the towing vehicle, the expertise and the efficiency is entirely in the trailer. For a while we used a hired unit which could pull the boat trailer and the reefers but the boat work continued to expand, therefore justifying the purchase of another unit. Dobbin had been purchased from D.J.Taylor Commercials, a truck dealer (and boat owner) so a replacement for Dobbin was sought from David's 'bargain basement'. A Volvo FL10 two-axle unit was acquired, which did give good service but had little personality and one major drawback; it had a single sleeper cab which resulted in some odd sleeping arrangements at times. Quite rightly 'Q' always believed that as he was the regular driver he had automatic right for the bunk. Fair enough. After all he had his gear in the cab and his sleeping bag was permanently installed. Where an attendant or second driver was required, it was therefore often necessary to beg the indulgence of the boat owners to allow one of us to sleep in the boat, promising of course to 'leave as we find'. This sometimes provided opportunities for being pampered in luxury and the boat mover's groupies were quality birds but often the accommodation was substandard and there were few visitors to these poor vessels.

Our first 'thousand pound day' where one job was started and completed the same day was the transfer of a lifeboat called 'Scubie-Doo' from Hartlepool to Milford Haven. It could, indeed should, have taken much longer but this day was one to 'tell your grandchildren about'. The achievement was even more impressive, because in those days escorts were provided by the police. They did not charge for the service but came when they could spare the time from other duties and escortable vehicles could be kept waiting for hours, even days.

Nowadays, escorting of abnormal loads is normally carried out by private contractors or some hauliers can justify providing their own. They charge of course, but they make our operations more predictable.

On this particular journey we were due to have police escorts on three separate stretches of road in different counties and also over the Severn Bridge. Usually, we would phone the police to advise of our readiness. Then we would wait. Then we might dare to phone again and would generally get the response that we are not a priority and we are not to keep ringing, or we go further down the order, or we find that the car allocated to us has been called away to take a colleague shopping, or to sit on a busy road and catch speeding motorists. So we wait. Then we calculate that it's after shift change so we phone again only to discover that nobody knows about us so the whole routine starts again. Then we get told off for pestering them so we give up. Eventually, we get the gas stove out, put the kettle on and make a brew. As the kettle comes to the boil, plod turns up and is in a hurry so expects us to move immediately. (Starting a brew earlier in the sequence would not achieve an early arrival.)

But this day would turn out to be different. The first escort kept us waiting for almost two minutes, the second one was waiting for us and we didn't have to stop and when we phoned to advise the third one of our impending arrival the force control said we could run unaccompanied after all. The Severn Crossing Authority sent a van to have a look at us and then allowed us to proceed. The M4 in South Wales, usually restricted with road works, for once was free flowing. We were doing well and were hoping to make Milford Haven in time for a pint, (this being company policy) a brilliant achievement considering the distance. But we hadn't accounted for the zeal of the boat owner.

We were low enough to get under Merlin's Bridge on the A4076 so we had the advantage of a shorter route to Milford Haven. But just south of Haverfordwest a car approached from the opposite direction with lights flashing. I suggested to 'Q' that it might have been the boat owner and a few minutes later the car overtook us, cut in sharply and drove ahead at a slower pace than we had

'Last Orders' Please

been achieving. The car, an Austin 'Allegro', was more like 'Rallantando' as it slowed further for each crossroads or road junction. An arm appeared at the driver's window and waved us frantically forward, urging us in the direction we had already chosen. "Last Orders at The Bar" were becoming an unlikely achievement as our new found guide (and guard) was determined to lead us to our destination. He was perhaps trying to impress his companions, three ladies looking less than comfortable with his erratic progress. As we slowly drove down the hill towards the turning, which would have taken us to the Milford Haven Marina Offices, Restaurant and Bar the car driver blocked our attempt to turn left and directed us to the other side of the dock. Somewhat miffed to miss 'last orders' we met our owner who proudly invited us to park there for the night. We responded with our hopes, now dashed, to get a pint at the marina pub. He realized the error of his ways, turfed his lady companions out of his car onto the quayside and drove us to the bar. We managed a couple of pints and perhaps a malt, before walking back to the vehicle. Neil retained his right to the bunk in the lorry and left me to suffer the discomfort of the steel floor of the lifeboat. To make matters worse Cameron Diaz stormed off in a huff having seen the inhospitable conditions!

The company policy of finishing each day with a pint or two was again sorely tested on the occasion of another trip to Milford Haven. Welsh drinking hours were inclined to be a bit variable with some places allowing plenty of opportunity and others succumbing to 'fire and brimstone' intimidation from the Methodists.

Late one Sunday night on the A40, 'Q' and I were running out of both safe parking opportunities and drinking time. Moreover, we were soon to run out of dual carriageway and we were not allowed on single-track roads in the dark. We passed a couple of lay-bys which were unsuitable and a restaurant closed and in darkness, passed a garage with a bit of space to park but very remote, then noticed a place with some streetlights on the other side of the road. As a last resort we parked where a lay-by had an extra area of space, apparently for school buses to park. Reasonable lighting and not far from St.Clears, this was the last chance for the night. 'Q' was in non-walking mode but was persuaded that there might be a pub still open at the village in the distance so we crossed the road, climbed over the fence and joined a lane which led towards the lights. There was not a soul about but there was a pub still open with a very friendly landlord. I think he was thrilled to have some company for we were his only customers. He served us good beer and joined us in a game of darts. Our situation had turned around for the better; from near disappointment to International Sports tournament.

"Good result," as they say.

The poor accommodation in the Volvo and the start of costly maintenance problems induced us to look for a double-bunked unit. A Daf CF 'Skycab' fitted the bill well enough and although it was second-hand it was well above the 'bargain basement'. It was somewhat of a quantum leap in that our cheaper units had been paid for and written off tax-wise, but this required a loan and when you have high overheads you have to keep the wheels turning. I use a saying which has more than a ring of truth; *"You can't make money with borrowed money."*

Anyway, our local Daf dealer supplied the unit and were authorised to undertake some jobs prior to our collection. The dealer was renowned for poor service and indifferent attitudes and our experiences served only to confirm and enhance this reputation. As we drove away from the Daf dealer we turned invisible. So, with some regret about the source of the vehicle we could at least sleep two persons in the lorry. But Dafs are very well made and the CF served us well just as long as we kept away from the dealer. On the rare occasions where we needed to use their facilities their incompetence was nothing short of spectacular! But we are survivors, so despite their 'best' efforts, our boat work continued to develop and step by step it became our main activity.

In July 1997 we bought a second-hand 'Special Types' boat trailer on steel springs. Giving the stability and comfort of the boats absolute priority, we had the steel springs changed to air suspension and engaged a local trailer specialist in the village of Camerton to modernise the trailer throughout and convert it to 'Construction and Use' Regulations (don't ask!). (This business eventually became part of Britcom International and did ongoing modifications when we found ways to improve the trailers). Although we were initially in no hurry this took around nine months longer than anticipated and our totally refurbished "Trailer Two" was ready for its new life in

May 1998. We kept the old axles to upgrade 'Trailer One' at a later date. As boat work increased we hired a unit to pull Trailer One so I was back on the boats again having earlier had to surrender that role to 'Q'. Eventually, there was enough work to justify another purchase.

We had a simple request to the dealers; "We need two-axles, air suspension, two bunks and a short wheelbase if possible". (The CF had such a long wheel base that there was room to have a dance between the back of the cab and the front of the trailer). David Taylor, our reliable supplier had plenty in the bargain basement but all were single sleepers. Eventually, from Andrew Justice in Derbyshire we found the true heir to Dobbin; compact, economical and easy to maintain!

This was 'Little MANdy'; twin sleeper, white top and pretty blue skirt, well shod and only four grand. No need for borrowings and ready for work.

MAN stands for Machinenfabrieken Auch Nurnburgen (or similar and not to be attempted by catarrh sufferers) so the initial letters would seem to be enough! The local MAN dealer was run by one of Paul's old schoolfriends (note Paul's input again) and we gave him the remit to look after our truck as if it were his own. Trailer One was upgraded using the axles inherited from trailer Two, a conversion not without serious problems but at least the payload was increased. Thus from October 2000 we had two units and two trailers almost exclusively on boat transport. As drivers left, agency work was discontinued and we no longer had refrigerated trailers. The next four or five years were perhaps the most comfortable period of all our years in business. Once the CF Daf was paid for and Little Mandy was inducted into the 'keels on wheels' regime, the business prospered.

Another of my philosophical observations goes as follows; "If you go chasing work in road haulage, there is

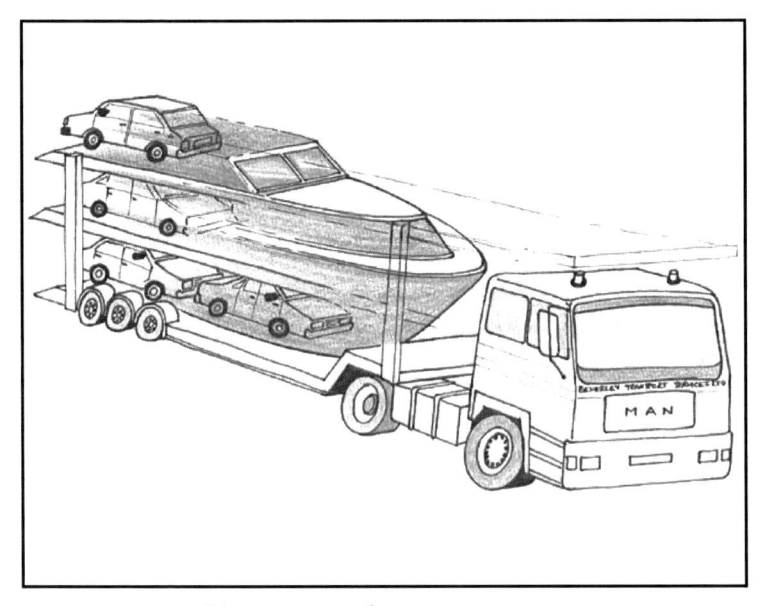

From car to boat transporter

always work to be found, but at someone else's rates." If work comes to you, you can price it up, present your case, emphasize the quality of your service not the lowest price, and hopefully win more deals than you lose!

So this was our 'business model'. From the quotes and offers available, plan a full week for 'Q'. Some of the jobs may be a bit iffy, but the earnings from one vehicle should cover overheads and Neil's wages plus a bit. Meanwhile Little Mandy was waiting, lurking in the shadows, ready to take on the last minute jobs, at the right price, hugely profitable of course. Well almost perhaps, well not really at all. Little Mandy got the destinations that the management favoured, especially Scotland! When you enjoy the job that you do, it's not work is it. Unoriginal but true.

Trailer Three was another ex-car transporter, this time a Rolfo Triple Decker. Ken Dale is a world-famous trailer engineering specialist who also happens to be a boat owner. Frequent conversations about our requirements, usually when moving his Princess V42 sports cruiser and Ken 'riding shotgun' set him on a mission to find a suitable unit. He found the near perfect type at Bruntingthorpe, a huge repository for cars, trucks, trailers and even planes that had been on charter in an earlier life. Purchased and top decks chopped off at a Hull scrapyard, the conversion work was shared between a local steel fabricators and Hairsine Trailers.

Backtracking a few years, Paul had been busy expanding his CV. Leaving the truck rental company with many contacts and acquaintances he joined us to look after the yard and develop his own valeting business. Applying his cleaning and polishing skills to other people's vehicles seemed a logical progression and he built up a steady flow of work with some 'blue chip' customers. When there were gaps he would undertake yard work; cleaning and checking our vehicles, stacking the hundreds of Tetra-tainers that disgorged from the fridges on the milk run each day and keeping an eye on the drivers.

On the day he came of age, there was but one target for Paul, his HGV licence! He could already manoeuvre with dexterity and the road work came as second nature, so he was soon manipulating and coercing us to get him his own vehicle. It may not have been quite 'state of the art' but the Rolls Royce engined ERF was Paul's pride and joy. They were a hard-working team and that motor would fly. I borrowed it once to do a boat job and found myself speeding on the A17 at almost twice the HGV speed limit. We had another ERF for a while too and 'Q' was a big fan. It is testimony to the skills of Mike Mcgwinn, the heroic, legendary ERF salesman that against all the odds he kept on succeeding in selling them until the factory stopped making them. He would turn any complaint on its head without so much as a blink of the eye.

"This heap of garbage is a flaming liability," or some such verbal abuse would be met with an encouraging riposte such as; "Mmm, perhaps, but it will never go rusty," or the even more frustrating, "Yes, but do you know that over eighty per cent of all the ERFs ever made are still registered at Swansea!"

But soon Paul persuaded us that we should be presenting a better image than these bargain basement lorries and so 'out of the pan into the fire', we traded in his ERF for a Renault, which had it not been under warranty, would probably have bust the company. But it was 'briny' and even starred in a wedding picture, when Paul married the lovely Susan Ripley. It lasted one day under a year, not the marriage, but the time we endured the Renault. Bad times hit us with a combination of greedy landlord, unhelpful bank and the need to 'downsize' the business, meant that we were overstaffed. We avoided redundancies but helped staff to leave when Natwest threatened to take the house.

There was never any doubt that Paul would find work as he had built up an excellent reputation through agency customers, rental company contacts and of course with his own vehicle. He took local work with a local animal feeds processor, known rather cynically as 'Splendid Blended' then moved to another local firm, Baxters. They found him another ERF with a Twin Splitter Gearbox (for those who understand and may be interested in these things) and he nurtured it until it was quite presentable. Paul then had a stint at a local pork factory, Cranswick Country Foods, so famous that it's even been mentioned in Parliament. We have had and still have, an enduring relationship with this business for work for our vehicles and drivers. Paul's work here sustained and enhanced his admiration for Scania trucks, but the work regime was not conducive to parenting. A return to local work with another animal feeds processor meant he could be at home at night after the birth of his son, Alex. But it would be a while before he came to enjoy the activity which he had instigated so many years before, the movement of boats. He had a stint on a skip lorry too; it would be rude to equate that with any sort of boat or boat owner among later activities. He then came back on the payroll in September 2008 shortly after starring in the Lads, Dads and Granddads Cricket Team at Center Parks, Penrith.

Little Mandy was a sickly lady at times. She suffered from a virus in her diesel tank which affected her circulation. On one occasion I had to call out a doctor on the A9 in the middle of winter and he soon cured the problem, but only for a while. The virus caused a stutter and weakening of Little Mandy's performance and we learned that it was incurable without a total transfusion of DERV and perhaps a pump and tank transplant. To make matters worse, she developed a grumbling gearbox which was incurable. While she could still move under her own power we sold her back to Andrew Justice and started the search once more for "Two axles, two beds, air suspension and short wheelbase. The economy was supposedly booming and the result was a shortage of any kind of reasonably priced second-hand lorry. There was no 'bargain basement' with anything over three years old being sold abroad. What units were available were as complicated as new ones and very expensive. This was to be a one and only, ever since time began event. We ordered a new truck!

Initially, this was not for the replacement of little Mandy but the Daf was getting to the point where trips back to the dealer were happening all too often and the dealer of course had a reputation to uphold. The visits became more frequent, took longer for less result and if the problems had been cured we would accept the cost with resignation but jobs were just never finished. So we sold the truck to Andrew Justice and implored him to find us another with 'two axles etc etc'. None were available for a while. So Mandy, our first and only new lorry was commissioned through Mike Mcgwinn the indomitable ERF salesman, now becoming converted to MAN as the German group took over that marque.

'Q' was chuffed to have a new truck, wanted it badged ERF but promised to stop smoking. Mandy's first outing was in January 2006. But for a good 'seam' of work, a new lorry would have been out of the question.

So, still needing a replacement for Little Mandy we pestered our contacts with our long standing requirements; two axles, two beds, air suspension and short wheel base.

Andrew Justice said "Well, I've got two out of four."
" How come?"

"Renault Premium, two axles, air suspension, long wheelbase, no beds, three seats!" Andrew explained that he had bought the assets of a Driver Training Business, including two units which had been converted for this purpose. Apart from extra pipework for dual control operation there was a third seat in the middle of the cab for the instructor. Bargain price, four grand plus a bit. You could say we had a good bit of history with the local Renault dealer. Paul had a 'work experience' stint with them many years ago and had been at school with lads who became their mechanics. The earlier near disaster with a Renault remained in our collective memory, but the French were beginning to make good trucks. I took my test with another Paul, a Mr. Collingwood even more years ago. He was and is Workshop Manager or even Engineering Director. Thus, we had men planted with the MAN dealer and the Renault dealer so we should be well looked after. But first 'Ronnie Rennow' as our new team member was to be called, needed to be made a bit more driver friendly.

One Saturday at the marina, Paul and Alex set about cleaning and polishing and I watched my workbench being used to make something practical for a change.

Alex was overheard to say, "Dressed like that, I don't think we'll get much work out of Grandad today!" The cheek of it, what I wear has nothing whatsoever to do with my incompetence, but very astute nevertheless! They made a bed too, and a mattress was obtained from a scrap Renault. A shortage of space for documents and bits and bobs, was remedied with the installation of a Trago Mills storage tray held in place with a brightly coloured bungee.

The spare seat came in useful for a project that Alex and I had shared, the making of a go-cart based on "The Dangerous Book for Boys". Our little machine now boasted an adjustable seat and seat belt, a cut above your average go-cart! Although this added comfort to the go-cart Alex was still concerned about the lack of brakes. I devised a system which had kitchen tiles attached to gate hinges with cables to increase the pressure, rubbing on the tyres. I bet it was the first go-cart *ever* to be fitted with *air-cooled ceramic brakes,* state of the art or what? That Saturday, thanks to Paul and Alex, I had a worthy replacement for Little Mandy.

Ronnie Rennow was a powerful beast, not without faults but did a good job with the boats. Whether his performance influenced Paul I will never know but eventually Paul eased me out of the driving seat and into the office more or less full time. Was there a master plan here? Ronnie was fast but functional and not the most glamorous lorry on the track. Also, he was not as reliable as any of our previous 'bargain basement' purchases nor as sure-footed! We hadn't suffered wheel spin since Dobbin's epic journey to Badachro but Ronnie Rennow's back end would twitch coming out of a roundabout, even on dry roads. He lacked the finesse of previous units and Paul began looking for a replacement, citing the slippery behaviour and potential serious malfunctions as justification. Ronnie was a bit of a maverick and was out of place in our team.

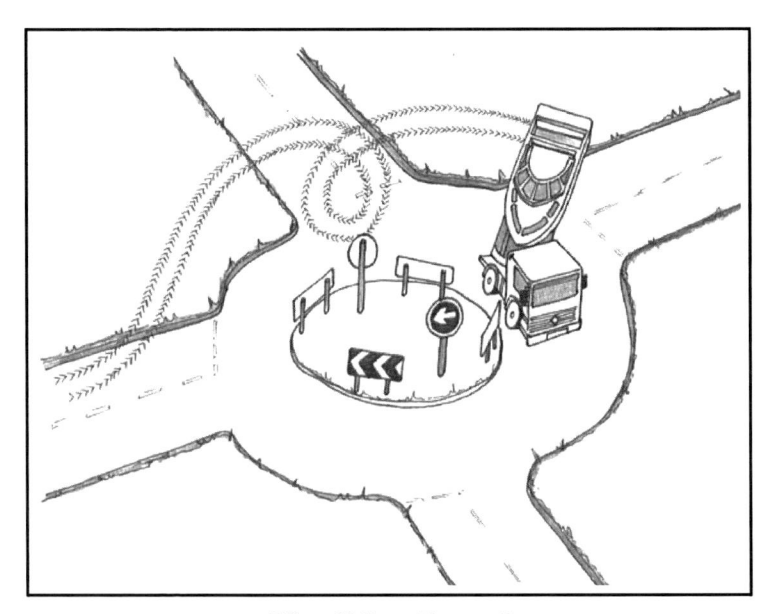

Slip-sliding Renault

Along came Dafney, a sophisticated lady with style and grace, capable of enhancing the fleet although she'd been round the block a few times. She could be a little bit skitty on the back end too, and had to be ballasted. Meanwhile Ronnie, who had been sold as a warehouse 'shunter', was seen charging down the A1 with tautliners and tilts. Reminding the purchaser that he had promised to remove the sign-writing, I was pleased to learn that Ronnie had found a new life where his brawn was appreciated. Meanwhile, Dafney gets hormone treatment as well as ballasting; the engine re-mapped and pump re-set. Still she skips and skids but Paul has the measure of her.

Paul's nickname at one of his previous jobs was 'Squeeky', earned through keeping his truck spotlessly clean. Dafney now gets the full works with shampoo and conditioner every week. Paul is now back at the venture he first instigated. As well as setting an example for Neil and I in terms of vehicle cleanliness and appearance, Paul has had his ear to the ground on more vital matters; the increasing powers of VOSA and the need for certain routines for 'compliance'.

We have always been thorough with maintenance but Paul tightened up our routines. The ten-minute walk round vehicle checks, the requirements for load restraint and the importance of record keeping routines were imposed on us old f****, with grudging but realistic acceptance. The tradition of customer care continues of course, but we must get up to date with 'networks' and 'systems.' Paul and Sue are dragging us kicking and screaming into the 21st Century. Our Fisher Price Computer and HB software are no longer up to the job!

CHAPTER TWELVE

Scotland's Wasted On You

You may have noticed that I have a great love for Scotland and some of the early boat jobs were to that beautiful country. When 'Q' took over on the boats it was galling for me to let him go up there when I could have gone instead. Never mind, the die was cast.

On one occasion whilst we still had Dobbin I asked him if he minded being 'weekended' away. There was a Broom 37 to take from Newark to Inverkip and it was to be delivered on the Saturday. Then there was a boat to collect from Ardfern on the Monday so the team would need to stay at Ardfern over the weekend. Neil agreed and took his brother Stuart as 'Second Man'. I envied them the opportunity to explore the area around Ardfern, an area noted for its fine scenery and sailing and famous through one of its sailors, Princess Anne. I had previously been a couple of times and had spent some time walking in the area.

I phoned Neil on the Sunday night and the conversation went something like this; "Hello, have you had a good weekend?"

"Not bad."

"Have you been down towards Aird and Craignish Point past Craignish Castle?"

"No"

"Have you been over the tops to Lunga and Craobhaven, that's a great walk?"

"No,"

"Have you climbed up to the lovely little lochs

behind Craigdhu?"

"No,"

"Have you been along the ridge on the far side of the marina, that's a pretty walk and easy going?"

"No,"

"Well, what have you done all weekend?"

"We've been in the pub watching football on the telly!"

"Well, Scotland's wasted on you. From now on I do the Scottish work!" And as far as possible I have always tried to engineer the jobs to enable me to carry out this pledge, as you may have noticed.

Whilst using the single bunked Volvo, we had occasion to head for the Isle of Skye to collect a fishing boat to take south to Newhaven. I double manned with 'Q' and we had a bit of revenue going North by taking the rusty shell of a steel yacht from Whitby to Renfrew. Whilst unloading we were soaked by a storm and stained by the rusty water bouncing off the boat. We needed somewhere to shower and somewhere for me to sleep. Following the obvious route towards Crianlarich we were soon made to realize our mistake. From Tarbet to Ardlui the road is barely passable for a lorry, even when empty and we made very slow progress. There was nowhere to park in Crianlarich so we turned west towards Glencoe but soon came across the hamlet called Tyndrum, which turned out to be a remarkable place in more ways than one.

Here we found a garage to purchase diesel, a shop called the Green Welly where we could stock up on essentials like fags, milk and tea bags, plus there was a decent lorry park at the back. Trying to obtain a room at the pub, we were directed to the 'Bunkhouse', a collection of timber buildings including a shop, restaurant, swimming pool and Post Office and bunks which were charged at £6 per night if you had your own sleeping bag. We enjoyed a great night in the pub, spoiled somewhat by midge attacks.

Neil claims he never would have eaten outside but for my insistence but still had a good night's sleep. This would be the first of many visits to this delightful little place, although sadly, the Bunkhouse is now long gone. For all its remote location Tyndrum boasts two railway stations, Tyndrum 'Upper' and Tyndrum 'Lower' still both in use. Believe it or not a gold mine was recently re-opened there too!

The sleeping arrangements on Skye were decidedly less comfortable. The job revolved around the collection of a Lochin 33 fishing boat which operated off the Isle of Harris. Its performance from new had been well below par and the boat was to be transported to the home of Lochins at Newhaven for assessment and improvement. The fisherman's costs were being met in part with a grant from the HIDB. We met at Uig, a small port on the north-west coast of the Isle of Skye. Neil is fond of reminding me and anyone else within earshot that when we boarded the ferry at the Kyle of Lochalsh I was driving and misheard the instructions shouted by the ferry crew resulting in the handbrake being ripped off the back of the trailer.

We proceeded to Uig, marvelling at the wonderful Red Hills and Black Cuillins (well, at least I noticed the fabulous scenery, Neil was unmoved by it). The boat was loaded onto our vehicle by a hired crane, the only one on the island apparently. We had to wait until the next morning for a police escort which meant sampling the fare provided by the bar on the pier. I have never seen so much whisky consumed in such a short period of time and a great atmosphere prevailed but I was unable to get too involved. Unfortunately, I had somehow drawn the short straw and would be the first driver in the morning.

'Q' has skills of almost genius standard for stating and justifying his role and if ever anything goes wrong he has his excuse ready before he has been asked for an explanation. He had somehow engineered things to leave

Singing and Snoring

me to take the first turn at the wheel the next morning. Thus I was only able to consume a modest amount of alcohol. Neil's profound and deeply humbling saying; "You can't do enough for a good boss" applied here and again he carried out his philosophy. When sleeping arrangements were discussed 'Q' offered to keep the lorry bunk to himself and leave me to endure the indignity of the fishing boat cabin which the crew insisted would accommodate three persons! But first they would make supper!

By now it is well after midnight and we withdrew from the bar. The two fishermen, Neil and I climbed onto the boat. They started playing tapes of Country and Western music; "Ooh I've been away and I shouldn't have left so I'm coming home to Yooooo," or words to that effect, wailing out across Uig harbour and village. Meanwhile, out comes the Fray Bentos! I have been in many fishing boats and the Fray Bentos 'cook in the tin' cuisine seems almost ubiquitous. Here on Skye, we're stood on the deck of the boat, drinking cans of beer, singing Country and Western songs (very badly) and I'm the party pooper wanting to get some sleep.

"But first ye'll need some supper and the meal will be ready in abooot an ooor!"

"No thanks, I'll retire if you don't mind"

Eventually, leaving the rest of them to await the completion of the cooking or the explosion of the Fray Bentos tin, I went below to the cabin. The 'bunks' were no more than planks slotted into the forward part of the boat. Bodies would therefore be arranged in a triangular, interlocking shape and if one person moved, everybody moved. Getting up for a pee disturbed the other two and returning from having a pee had the same effect. Thus, each person having one outside 'visit' caused six disturbances multiplied by three, meant a possible eighteen disruptions in the cramped space if we each got up only once. Not the best night's sleep for me but as long as Neil was OK (looking after the staff being so important) and eventually morning came to end the ordeal. The police arrived to escort us off the island and whilst waiting for clearance to pass through Broadford we were engaged in conversation with the lady officer. She said her brother was buying a passenger launch (with a grant from the HIDB as if you didn't know) to ferry passengers from the mainland to a hotel on Skye. I gave her a card and a couple of weeks later 'Q' brought the boat to The Kyle Of Lochalsh. Good salesmanship or what!

The Lochin was duly modified at Newhaven; apparently the 'shaft angle'was the cause of the restricted performance (surely a very common ailment) and whereas previously the boat managed a maximum of fourteen knots, now it would do seventeen! Wow! I don't think the HIDB had value for money out of that trip but they didn't seem to care. The fisherman flew to Newhaven to undertake sea trials and travelled back north as "second man". 'Q' was due to start his holidays so we swapped over near Preston on the M6 and I continued the journey to Uig. Perhaps I had engineered the timing to ensure 'Q' was away, thus providing myself with another trip to Scotland. Who knows? Who cares?

Amongst the frenzy of privatizations in the 80s and 90s (telephones gas, etc. Remember the 'Tell Sid' campaign) one received little publicity. The public toilets at the ferry terminal at the Kyle of Lochalsh were taken over by an enterprising individual who improved the facilities and decorated the premises with tourist pictures and brochures, installed showers and hairdriers, all for an entrance fee of ten pence. This was done without the help of the HIDB and provided welcome relief for people in the queue for the ferry. How has it fared since the Skye Bridge was built, I wonder?

Approaching Uig Harbour on Saturday afternoon, we were slowed by a figure walking somewhat unsteadily towards us. He was staring intently at the boat and waving at us to stop. I duly obliged and wound down the window.
"Is that in the sale?" he asked either in Gallic or more likely 'Alcoholic' for I couldn't grasp his question. My companion knew a bit of both languages and discerned that there was an auction taking place nearby and our inquisitor thought the boat was perhaps going under the hammer.
"It's good crack!" he asserted, meaning I think that either there were some good items in the auction or perhaps that everybody concerned was having a good time. As we were not due to be craned into the water until Monday it seemed like a good idea to have a look at the function if only to kill a bit of time. The auctioneers had assembled items from all over the island and it was a major event for the community with side stalls and a snack bar. Roughly every thirty minutes or so the auctioneer would

indicate a pause in the proceedings and most people took advantage of the adjournment to visit the bar on the pier. It might have been worth a bid for some of the items. There was a 1952 Wolseley car, several Mercedes vans and plenty of builders tools and equipment. My eye was taken by a weigh scale, of the type you used to see on railway stations; bright red with all the wonderfully intricate brass workings visible through a clear glass face. But this was commercial, not the "I Speak Your Weight" variety. The platform was pallet sized and the kit would obviously be used for weighing fish or other palletised products. It would have made a spectacular garden ornament to complement our 'phone box!

Alas, the bidding went way out of my league and the scales fetched over seven hundred pounds. Perhaps the purchaser of the Wolseley or one of the vans would be looking for transport to take their goods away. No such luck.

The adjournments took their toll as fewer people returned from the bar and those who did return were increasingly inebriated. The event was entertaining if not profitable and it filled in some waiting time. Sunday was occupied by walking and Monday morning by the craning of the fishing boat into the water.

Some journeys just failed to reach Skye, being terminated at the Kyle of Lochalsh. One trip with a fishing boat was from Bridlington and the owner 'rode shotgun' quite appropriate really as he was an ex-forces specialist who had earned a lump of money in Iraq and had bought the boat with the proceeds. We camped at Dalwhinnie en route and as it was winter time our SAS man booked a room for himself and his mate at the hotel. The lorry park has long since gone but at the time there was still a good parking area within easy walking distance of the bar. Sadly, at the time of writing the hotel is closed and boarded up.

Scotland has some delightful little harbours most of which were carved from hostile surroundigs by our forebears. Eyemouth, the Berwicks, Pittenweem, Anstruther, Arbroath, Stonehaven, Banff, Buckie, Lossiemouth, Burghead and Finhorn are steeped in fishing history, being home to fishermen who braved the hostile North Sea for a living. Though the oil industry has changed some of them, many more have adapted to serve the leisure industry. In particular, our friends, the Wafis, can add to their martyrdom by sailing these cold unfriendly, inhospitable waters.

However hard I tried to fulfil my pledge to keep the Scottish work to myself I sometimes had to let 'Q' go, however disappointing it was for me and however unfullfilling Scotland was for him. Some jobs we could do together and on one such trip we discovered Craobhaven, a modern marina in a modern village made to look old and quaint. It works!

One of our most long lasting friends and customers is Goodchild Marine Sevices run by Sue and Alan Goodchild at Burgh Castle, Great Yarmouth. Professional, efficient lovely people, they work to exceptionally high standards and have hired us for some very interesting jobs. I went with Mad Max to deliver a highly sophisticated workboat to the Aberdeen Harbour Authority with state of the art, early GPS equipment. Some time later I had to concede to 'Q', a trip to the Shetlands with a Goodchild product. The Sullom Voe harbour authority insisted on their workboat being delivered dry so Neil took Alan as 'second man' which enabled him to commission the boat too. My anguish at missing the trip was somewhat alleviated when 'Q' phoned to say they were delayed at Aberdeen due to gales. The ferry came in to port listing to port at an angle of fourteen degrees. Quite a storm! I am not a good sailor so fate had played a good hand for once.

Ferry listing

The job was completed, Alan flew home and Neil worked his way back to England.

Another lapse of my concentration enabled 'Q' to deliver a boat to Caley Marine at Inverness. While he was there, he was hijacked by Jamie to collect a cruiser from the Kyle of Lochalsh. That's just rubbing it in! Gradually my grip on the Scottish trips was being relaxed and 'Q' had a number of journeys with "Coastworker" a workboat chartered out by Coastworks of Largs.

I did manage some visits which combined good business with the joy of visiting the country. Scotland is full of surprises and the fickle weather conducts an ever-changing drama on the landscape. One Saturday in the merry month of May I travelled through Spey-side to reach Findhorn, on the coast, east of Inverness. The land looked dry as a bone and people were watering their gardens, this in one of the wettest parts of the British Isles! At Findhorn the people in the pubs had spilled out onto the streets and the slopes down to the water's edge. The scene was more Mediterranian than 'Morayvian'. The cruiser was due to be loaded on the Monday morning but having negotiated the narrow streets I found the boatyard and was able to load on the Saturday afternoon. I was then free to enjoy the good weather and continue my Scottish investments by sampling some local malt whiskies. The evening was completed with a walk in the near daylight conditions around the beautiful bay at midnight.

A day ahead of plan, I should have gone exploring on the Sunday around Findhorn but chose to head south for Plymouth with the Moonraker cruiser. Quiet roads, sunshine and time to meditate.

Another trip to the Moray coast was to nearby Burghead. I took Carl, our "second man" at the time and arrived in the quaint village quite late at night. There was nowhere to eat but a friendly pub had good music and a liquid supper was imbibed. The crane arrived at an unheard of time of five-thirty in the morning and we were off to Aberdeen to collect a Trader cruiser. No time to explore Burghead, which was a shame. The trip was spoiled by a minor disaster. Neil swapped with me at Lymn Truckstop on the M6 and shortly after an airbag blew on the trailer causing slight damage to the keel of the boat and a very awkward roadside repair. But as we often say, "We live to fight another day!"

An urgent call from a crane driver from Adrishaig at the southern end of the Crinan Canal sent me hurrying to help recover a Colvic Watson Yacht which was laying on the towpath at the side of the canal near Lochgilphead. Apparently, having been for sale for over a year, and not finding a buyer, the yacht had mysteriously self combusted.

An attempt to remove it from the canal ended in disaster for the crane was not up to job and the craft could

Fire damage sale

only be dragged onto the towpath. Worse still, the crane was trapped behind the boat. Our Iain came along as "second man" and we drove up overnight one Friday arriving in Adrishaig just after dawn. After a short sleep we met the crane driver, travelled to the site and began the task. Another crane turned up and between us we succeeded in lifting the burned out shell. By the end of the morning, blackened from the charred remains of the inside of the boat, we had the craft secured on the trailer. Inside was a pile of charcoal, a load of tangled wires and a more or less complete mast. All the bulkheads were burnt through and we had to improvise some 'splints' to serve as chocks to give the load some integrity. The load was ready to move and we parked on the ramp leading from the road to the canal side.

Brothers Paul and Iain are 'chalk and cheese' but I am fortunate in having some common ground with each of them. With Paul, it's always been vehicles; a milk float as a toddler, then cars and lorries. With Iain it's been music; keyboard for a birthday then guitars. In truth there's plenty of overlap, with the three of us enjoying Rock music. We also have a taste for good beer despite Iain's defection to lager.

Dirty, smelly and tired, Iain and I opted to leave the primitive accomodation of the cab and seek better facilities. First port of call, the Comme, a small bar devoted to what bars do best, serve drink! For anyone seeking a good philosophy for life, have a look at the messages engraved in the mirrors around the little bar area. Thirst slaked, we moved along the street to book a room at the Argyll Hotel, reserving Room Two. This was at a special price for 'working people' as the manager described us, but cheap because it was above the disco, and on Saturday nights the place was flooded with young people from the surrounding area and would be somewhat noisy. We were promised the 'best breakfast in Argyll' and we made ouselves at home. I crashed out early and heard nothing of the disco but woke for a pee to see the street below filled with early morning revellers. Iain had enjoyed the disco, was difficult to waken but the breakfast fulfilled expectations.

At twelve foot wide, a police escort was required, which was booked to take place on the Monday morning but as we were ready to go I asked if we could move on the Sunday. We waited on the canal side and the patrol car arrived. One officer got out and spoke to us.

"My Inspector has joined us to see how this escorting lark is done," he said with an expression which might have indicated disapproval or anxiety.

It's our policy to stop after a couple of miles to check the load and therafter at intervals depending on the nature of the boat. Yachts, like their owners are often troublesome in transit and this one was particularly fragile so I asked our escort if we could check the load during the journey.

First stop, just outside Lochgillphead, nothing untoward but the officer said that his superior expressed a view that the load looked wider than the twelve notified feet! It turned out that the timbers we had put in the hull to give it some rigidity were jerking downwards and widening the boat. Tightening the straps did not help! We continued our journey.

As we approached Inverary, looking in the mirror, I could see some of the tangled wires had decided to untangle themselves and spring over the side of the boat. Luckily the wires were on the nearside and could not be seen by the observant Inspector and at our next stop I managed to throw the wires back into the boat. We stopped at Tarbet for the night and continued to Essex the following morning. The load was now nearly fourteen feet wide and it was a tight squeeze to enter the boatyard. Who would buy that heap of blistered garbage I wondered. As I collected our cheque, a gentleman got out of an Austin 1800 and went to see about buying it! It takes all sorts I guess.

CHAPTER THIRTEEN
Classics & 'Wafis'

By definition, the term 'classic' refers to something of lasting merit, a recognised standard, a distinguished and permanent design or product. Classical music can be tedious, funereal and sleep inducing but it does reflect the definition. The 'classic' languages, Latin, Greek and Broad Yorkshire, follow established rules and systems and are perpetuated by scholars who can't be bothered to learn a modern language or who are bracing themselves for another Roman invasion or perhaps independence for 'God's Own County'.

Classic cars have a kind of magic or long lasting reputation and I suppose classic boats have a similar pedigree and therefore comply with the definition. So why should the words "She's A Classic You Know," cause a little anxiety for the boat haulier? To be fair, there are some genuine classic cars like the Mini, the E-Type Jaguar and the Ford Mustang and many pre-war motors.

Trailer One inherited the ramps from its first life as a car transporter. On odd occasions these were used, in this instance to collect a classic Ford Fairline, vintage circa 1956 in full hot climate condition, imported from Saudi Arabia via Tilbury docks. The car was destined for North Cave, a village on the edge of the Yorkshire Wolds, home of the owner. His presence was required at Tilbury to pay import duties and I asked if he wanted to ride down with me. Somewhat disdainfully he said he would go by plane adding that going south he would be using a Buccaneer and returning in a Tornado, both classic warplanes if you like!

Where he landed I never knew but it turned out his purpose was to take the Buccaneer for a windscreen replacement! Two planes plus Dobbin to collect one classic car for the chief test pilot of British Aerospace! He was somewhat miffed to find himself invisible when demanding the attention of the dockers.

The marine world also has it's classics but the definition becomes stretched at times. Men who served in the Second World War will rave about wooden craft made of classic 'Double Diagonal' construction. Many of the brave 'Little Ships' that went to Dunkirk are often referred to as classics and they are surely worthy of our admiration but there are just as many dubious or outright fraudulent vessels for which the term 'classic' is applied. Perhaps like 'beauty', classic is in the eye of the beholder, or perhaps sailor. Of greater relevance from our point of view are the integrity of the structure and the capability of the craft to endure being craned or hoisted onto the lorry, never mind its classic status. Some 'classics' are extremely fragile. A true classic and genuine Dunkirk veteran was 'Hilfranor', an exquisitely preserved timber boat. Bought by an ex-BA cabin attendant, whose voice was nine out of ten for Kenneth Williams - know who I mean? - this boat was moved several times between the Solent and the Thames. A walk on the deck permitted nothing more abrasive than socks as the gloss on the timber was of such high quality.

Some lottery money was made available around the turn of the century to set about the restoration of a number of classic forces boats from the Second World War. What started life as Admiralty Launches, used by the admirals to get from ship to shore, assumed various new roles during hostilities. The same design was used for Motor Torpedo Boats, Air Sea Rescue launches and even the army had some for amphibious landings. We had the privilege to collect several of these craft from disparate locations and deliver them to Marchwood for the attention of the restorers, some of whom were the original craftsmen, brought out of retirement for this project.

"I've got a Morecambe Bay Prawner, she's a classic you know."

I assumed this referred to a commercial craft, named according to its location and function and therefore would be a fishing vessel, sturdy and solid. When the owner asked for prices to take it from Conway to Milford Haven for a series of races I was a little puzzled. Would it be chasing or racing the prawns, competing with other similarly named vessels to catch a certain number of prawns in a given time, or what? It turned out to be a truly 'classic' sailing boat, beautifully built of wood and requiring extra special care and handling!

I reckon these terms; Crabber, Shrimper, Cockler and Prawner are names purloined by yachties to convince their wives they were off trying to earn a living, whereas all the time they were playing. Imagine the homecoming greeting; "Where do you think you've been all day?"

"Oh, I just popped out in our classic Cornish Shrimper to try to land our supper dear."

"So, where is it?"

"Where is what?"

"Our shrimp supper."

"Oh, sadly the shrimps weren't biting today."

Some motor cruisers are afforded the tile of 'classics' sometimes just by their owners, sometimes by common consent. The Norfolk Broads spawned a number of builders for both sailing and powered boating. A character from Bradford called me to quote for bringing a pre-war wooden Broads cruiser, "she's a classic actually", from Brundall Bay Marina to Fallwood Marina between Leeds and Bradford. Arriving at Brundall Bay to load early one Friday afternoon I found Mark and Shaun concerned about the risk of lifting this boat. They required a signed disclaimer from the owner who was not in attendance but was apparently on his way. Several phone calls at intervals suggested he was becoming more distant rather than closer. Somewhat puzzled, I asked for his location.

"I don't know I'm looking for a garage."

"Why, are you short of fuel?"

"No, my exhaust has dropped off and I need to get it fixed."

"Do you know whereabouts you are, are you on the A47?"

"No, I'm in Norwich I think, looking for a Skoda agent."

At that time ownership of that make of car was cause for derision and was the source of many jokes, and the eventual arrival of the owner confirmed the impression.

"There is concern that the boat may bend when in the slings of the hoist, so they would like you to sign a disclaimer."

"No problem, this boat is sound as a pound, a classic you know!"

Form duly signed, boat lifted on to trailer, preparations for transport started.

Many Broads' craft have various devices to lower their cabins to go under Potter Heigham Bridge. Some slide, some fold, this was the original 'flat pack'. As the owner and I started to fold it down, the whole thing collapsed with breaking glass and cracking of timbers. Undeterred, he kicked the debris down below.

"Glass can easily be replaced," he said dismissively. I tidied up as best I could for now it was dark. The owner left, still seeking the elusive Skoda dealer.

Driving along the A17 on the Saturday morning I became concerned about the view in the mirror. It looked like thick dust was blowing out of the front of the boat. I stopped to discover gaping holes in the sides. As the

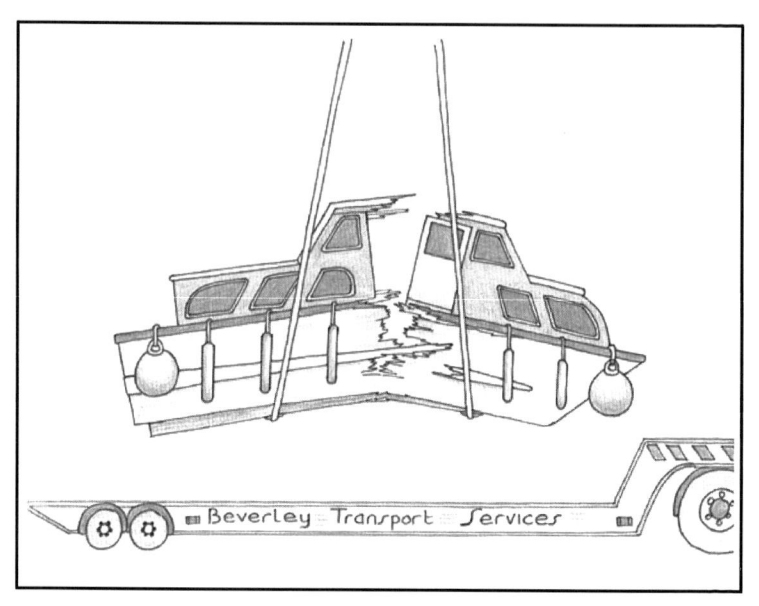

A Classic for sure!

timbers were drying out they were crumbling and powdering and by the time I reached Fallwood the boat was somewhat skeletal.

The lift was booked for nine-thirty on the Monday morning. Crane, lorry, boat and marina staff were all present, but again, no sign of the owner. Was he still looking for the Skoda dealer? No, he had forgotten where he was supposed to be! Finally, he turned up and although he looked a bit puzzled at the perforated hull of the boat, he helped to hold the slings against the sides. I asked him to explain the thinking behind this project.

"Well you see, I restore classic motor-bikes, so I thought I would have a go at a classic boat!"

Fairey motor cruisers are genuine classics, the range developed by the coming together after the war of aviation experts who built craft of impressive performance and beauty. Gavin Poole, a broker at Poole specialises in these classics and on his behalf we have moved several examples of the Fairey Huntsman, Swordsman and

Swordfish. One of our customers with a classic Huntsman, *"Ischia"* contracted us first to move it from Largs to Poole, then to Bristol. It's colourful history confirmed it's genuine 'classic' status having once been owned by a diplomat, a friend of Ian Fleming. The resulting association led to the speedboat scene at the end of 'From Russia With Love' starring of course, Fairey speedboats.

Norseman '38' cruisers have a unique if not truly classic history. They were originally built as open passenger boats to transfer cruise line passengers from liner to port where there were no harbour facilities. They were ruggedly built to be beached at speed to allow passengers to disembark. Some have found a new life fitted out as pleasure cruisers. The hull looks like an ice-breaker with a steel blade at the front of the keel. The hull is heavily protected and the shafts are enclosed in armoured tubes. Fortunately, the layout of our trailers permits the fairly easy loading of these uniquely tough hulls. The added superstructure and fitting out has produced a boat of distinguished character. Our friend Brian keeps moving his to new locations, for which we are very grateful. Another was owned by 'Dredger Steve' a chap with a Far Eastern bride who we moved around to where his company was working.

'Q' has often claimed that his overalls should be embroidered "By Appointment to the Aristocracy" because he had the responsibility of bringing a classic Gentlemen's Thames Cruiser from Windsor to York. This was by the patronage of the Honourable Simon Howard of Castle Howard, the country seat of the Howard family whose house was used for the filming of 'Brideshead Revisited' and other classic programmes. As I write, Trailer One is host to this cruiser as it undergoes restoration work in a barn on the Castle Howard Estate.

Mind you, the Admiral 'Q' is a bit less vociferous about another of his clients whose trawler yacht he took from Torquay to the Clyde. "I Love the Krankies," on your overalls doesn't have quite the same kudos does it, but good customers nevertheless.

A wooden cruiser, beautifully restored in a two-year period was not only a genuine classic but the siting of the restoration work made the job rather unusual. In February 1998 'Q' took a rather tired looking Stanilands cruiser from Beverley to Hawes, high in the Yorkshire Dales National Park and about as far away from cruising water as you could get. Comments about the owner taking global warming and the rising sea level too seriously fell on deaf ears. In April 2000 I collected it, now in absolutely mint condition, the boat, not me, and took it home to Thorne where it had been built. After the weekend spent here for enthusiasts to view and reminisce, it was re-launched at Grimsby.

I was asked to collect a Spray, to *some* a classic triple-keeled yacht from Fleetwood and deliver it to an industrial estate near RAF Finningley, now part of Robin Hood Airport. Things are a bit different at Fleetwood now but at the time they had a crane for lifting the boats and the storage yard was maybe 200yards away. The Spray had been on its mooring, not moving, for over fifteen years and when it emerged from the water it was festooned with the most evil growths I have ever seen. I christened it 'Bin Laden's Germ Warfare Factory' and declared; "There's no way that festering heap is going on my trailer until it's clean!" or words to that effect. Whilst Pete Smith and his team sympathised, they pointed out that the steam cleaner was in the yard and the only way to get the boat to the machine was on my trailer. The slimy mass was duly lowered thereon. To attach the support pads I had to scrape away the growth with a spade, clearing enough to provide a 'cleanish' contact. The mucous-like mass was made up of nests of thick worms, which spat or extruded a sticky fluid when touched. Before the steam cleaner could clear

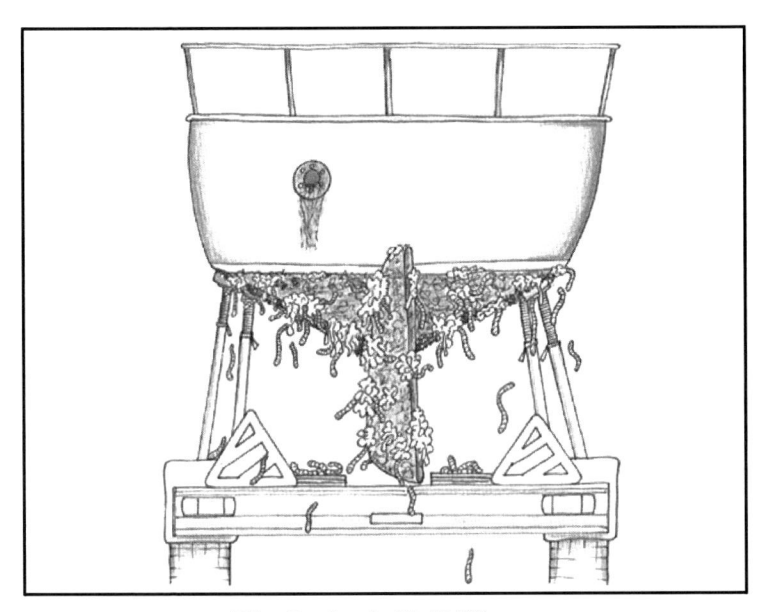

Bin Laden's Evil Worms

the mess, many of the nests dropped onto the trailer and the evil beasties started growing in the corners and crevasses. When I unloaded the next day it took the rest of the morning to make the trailer more or less presentable but the worms kept appearing for days.

From imagined or invented '*classics*' we turn to '*wafis*', a term to describe people with yachts. It could stand for 'Wise and Fair Informant' but it doesn't. It could stand for 'Warm and Friendly Individual' but it doesn't. It could stand for 'Wild and Fierce intentions' but it doesn't. It stands for 'wind assisted' and I'm not sure about the rest. We should not abuse these people. Despite their reluctance to use our services and their assertion that wind power is much more efficient than diesel, they can nevertheless, sometimes become customers. This 'flag and stick' brigade are mainly lovely people but they do tend to have their heads either buried in the sand or more likely, up in the clouds. I think most boat hauliers would agree that no amount of scheming, diligent pricing or meticulous load planning will ever justify the hassle that is generally involved when trying to move yachts. Some of the owners seem to believe that as the wind is free, so should everything else, including road transport.

Paul drew the short straw with a couple of dedicated sailors moving from a marina on the Clyde to the Tyne. The initial enquiry centred round a fin keeled yacht 'less than thirty feet long'. When asked for the beam it would be 'about eight foot or so'. (Remember Raymond's Rule; when in the pub, sixty foot long and twenty feet wide. When coming to pay, twenty foot long and six foot wide.)

So, when checking dimensions, it's nine foot ten on the beam, notifiable. But it shouldn't cause problems with escorts etc. So, quote given as per specification.

Then, "Ooh, there's a trailer to go too, if that's OK. It can just lay behind the boat."

"How big is it?"

"Oh, it's made to collapse so it won't be a problem."

"We'll try to accommodate it then."

"Ooh, nearly forgot, there are some masts off another boat to go too." And here we could add "etcetrabloomingetcetera!"

Paul arrived to commence loading and looked at their trailer. It turned out to be as big as our artic trailer, but never mind, we could take it to pieces, the 'we' being the assumption that Paul would do most of the dismantling. The pieces weighed a ton but had to be lifted by hand, no crane being available. Paul, with a bad back, made worse by the efforts got some light relief watching another WAFI launch his boat down the slipway. You could read the words from his cocky demeanour.

"Look at me folks, I can do it myself, don't need a haulier to move my boat nor a hoist to launch it. Allow me to demonstrate."

So he stopped at the top of the slipway, unfastened the retaining straps, strolled casually back to the car in the

Boat 'slipped' away

Berghaus top, slacks and Timberland Deck Shoes and got in. He slowly reversed down the slope. Boat floated. Driver looked around for audience approval of such skill. Meanwhile, boat floated away. Calm demeanour changed to panic. Waded in after yacht. Berghaus and Timberland tackle very soggy.

    The yacht, the 'collapsible' trailer the masts and all the other junk were finally loaded and looked like a travelling circus with all Paul's straps, ropes, bungees and clips all pressed into service. With all this important, even vital stuff safely delivered to Tyneside, a word of gratitude or at least an acknowledgement for the care taken would be the least to be expected. But no, all the stuff around the yacht was going to be weighed in for scrap!

    "Will I need to lower the mast?" is not a FAQ, to use a 21st century abbreviation, but it has been asked more often than you would imagine. Believe it or not, some yachties have no concept of the height of bridges, power and telephone lines nor the dimensions of the craft they sail on.

A typical conversation with a WAFI might proceed thus, "Good Morning, how much to take my yacht to Hartlepool?"

"Where is it now?"

"Oh, on the Solent"

"Whereabouts on the Solent?"

"Er, Southampton"

"Which marina, it could affect the price?"

So, eventually we find out more or less where the boat is and I will quote a range of prices, the maximum for the cost of the full round trip and the minimum on the basis that this could be a 'return' or 'back'load. I will emphasize that a price somewhere in between the two is a more realistic scenario. In reality, all loads are now 'return' loads.

Unfortunately, there is a ratio of around six or eight northbound loads to every southbound journey and matching up traffic is never easy. Indeed, we tend to zig-zag to and from different waterways to save on mileage and achieve some kind of efficiency. The work could be considered either price sensitive or time sensitive but Wafis want a cheap price and they want it now!

Pick any of the following responses;

W. "I'll have the back load price please and I would like the boat collecting on Monday morning"

Me. "Ah, but that would not constitute a return load as we couldn't take an outward load and be ready for you on Monday morning. Perhaps Tuesday or Wednesday of that week would enable us to match it up".

W. "Oh No, that's no good. We finish sailing on Sunday so we need it bringing back on Monday or we will have to pay extra nights' mooring charges!"

Or;

W. "Huh, I'm not paying any of that, I'll sail it back

with my mate"

Me. "Well, just think on, if you get to Brighton and then call us it will be an extra hundred pounds, if you get to Ramsgate then call us it will be another hundred again." The caller is now becoming irate.

W. "How can you say that then?"

Me. "Well, you'll set off from Southampton with your best mate, having promised him a week's joyful sailing . . . He's shortly to become your ex-mate because he's been soaked with rain and spray, chilled by the damp cabin and abused by you, "cos I'm the skipper and you're just a deck hand and anyway it's my boat", making him do all the dirty jobs, dangle his backside in the water. . . he's sat in the same soggy clothes for three days . . . the North Easterlies will blow you back down the Channel . . . and finally, you'll have to pay to repatriate him to his sane friends and family when he runs out of the valuable holiday that he has wasted crewing for you!"

Obviously some would dispute the above account but I can assure you that it has happened, and more than once with yachts later recovered from anywhere between Brighton and Ipswich.

Or,

W. "You did the same move for my friend and you charged him much less than that."

Me. "When was that then?"

W. "A few years ago, I'm not sure when."

No comment.

Or,

W. "OK, We'll go for that price but we'll have it put on a farm where they'll let me keep it for the winter."

Me. "What about access to the farm? Is it a proper road? Are there low trees? Have you costed crane hire and checked availability? These things will affect the price."

W. "Oh no, we agreed a price, why the extra?"

Or,

W. "If we accept your price we'd like to leave it on your trailer for a couple of days so we can anti-foul it before it goes in the water."

Or,

W. "The mast is laid next to the boat so your driver can lift it onto his trailer?"

When the driver finds it, there are wires spread everywhere, the speed log is broken or the lights are about to fall off and he is expected to lift the whole untidy mess onto the trailer on his own. Even when the mast is laid on the deck, which is the ideal location, there is often a need for the driver to change the location or add insulation.

Shrink wrap and duct tape, judiciously applied in liberal quantities will not only tidy up the mast and its cumbersome attachments but if used generously enough, will take the wafi weeks to undo at the other end of the journey.

On one occasion, having loaded a thirty-eight foot yacht at Largs, we looked around for the mast. No luck in the marina so we rang the owner.

W. "Oh yes, forgot to tell you, the mast's next door"
Me. "How do you mean, next door?"
W. "You know, the next marina."
Me. "In which direction?."
W. "Er, at Clyde Marina."
Me. "That's at Ardrossan, about twelve miles away!"
W. Yes, next door!" We duly presented ourselves at Clyde Marina and despite them not having had notice, they were prepared to lift the mast onto the boat. There had been no preparation, all the wires and stays fell about the boat and we had to recover the situation unaided, a risky situation created by the unthinking Wafi. He did not expect to pay any more for time and inconvenience stating; "Well, Ardrossan was on your way back to Liverpool anyway!" The cheek of it.

A useful phrase to use when negotiations are

becoming fraught is, "Well, we may not be the best but we're probably the most expensive!"

It tends to focus the mind and occasionally induce a reaction.

How about this for a recent enquiry, conducted through e-mails, the modern impersonal means of communication?

The request was for a *fin* keeled yacht to be loaded on the coast and taken to a farm in the Midlands. No place names, just postcodes were given. I checked the details on line, discovered it was *bilge* keeled and that the place to load had no lifting facilities. I e-mailed the enquirer, noting the above points, asked how he proposed to load and unload it and got this reply;

"Hi, yes it is a bilge keel. Not sure how fin keel came up. If I can find someone in the community to lift it, say two-foot off the ground, can your trailer back under it to load it? Neighbour of mine has a giant telescopic crane used for bungee jumping. Beast of a crane but not sure what kind of lifting sling and frame is needed. Any ideas? Perhaps I could obtain some girders from a nearby builder's demolition yard and bolt one together. Several farmers have telescopic handlers, but not sure if they are up to it."

The enquirer then went on to describe 'a difficult entrance' etc.

'Right fair, isn't it just like knitting fog!'

It would be unfair to tar all sailors with the same Wafi brush for there are some remarkably normal and very co-operative sailors who we are pleased to work with. The Peacock family, to modify a modern term are perhaps 'the acceptable face of wafis' with a strong tradition of sailing and who have provided us with numerous yacht movements over the years. Andy, in particular has bought

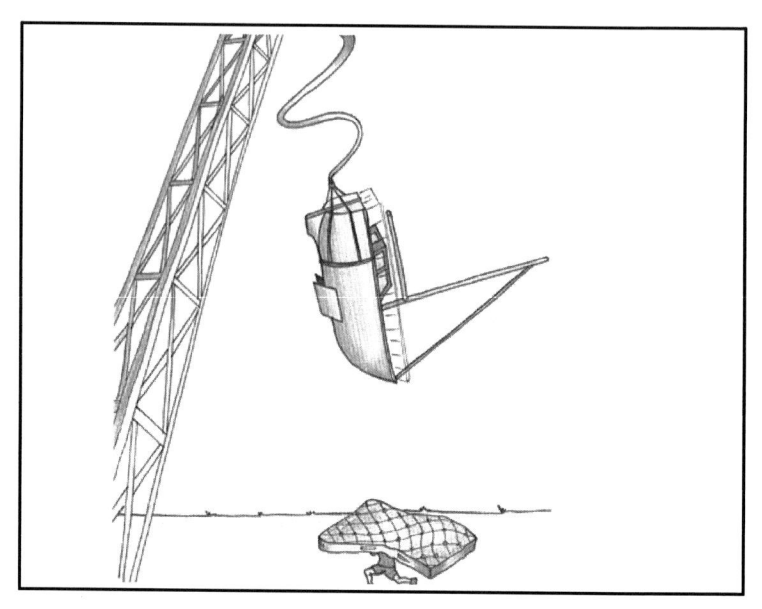

Bungee jumping yacht

and sold several yachts which we have been privileged to move. Fortunately, having a certain understanding of road transport and being aware of some of our experiences, Andy generally arranges things to be fairly straightforward. So there's not much point in putting him in this book then is there? But even he can't be blamed for one of our most recent Wafi delays. Loaded at Inverkip, Paul set off for Hull around six in the morning with a new yacht for Andy, became stranded by floods at Greenock at twenty past and sat there until mid-morning the following day, a total of twenty-eight hours. No chance of recovering losses on this one.

Some years ago, Andy rescued the owner of a Birchwood TS37 and his boat. Holed below the waterline, perhaps on the causeway used by the Romans to cross the Humber, the boat was in danger of sinking. Andy drove it at full speed up the river bank at Brough and provided us with another recovery job.

Keep 'em coming Andy!

"I'll be racing at Blyth, finishing around fifteen hundred hours on Friday afternoon, entering the hoisting area at Royal Quays by seventeen hundred hours and be racing on the Solent by ten hundred on Saturday! Any problems? How much?"

After much head-scratching and chin stroking 'Q' and I worked out how we would have to work within the driver's hours regulations, and we agreed prices with Peter, the bustling owner. Our target was to be away from the Tyne by six-thirty but it was nearer eight 'o' clock by the time we left in the mist.

'Hummingbird' was a racing yacht and was prepared for transport by the energetic crew including a very agile young lady who was winched up the mast to unstep the rigging or whatever yachties mean when they take the mast down. Royal Quays then hoisted her (the boat not the girl) onto our trailer. Stopping at intervals to check the load, we travelled south. At one point we were passed by a large Mercedes car with a girl hanging out of the window making a video. Yes, it was the acrobatic crew member and maybe Peter's girlfriend. We arrived at Hamble Point around six thirty, job done in good time. We have subsequently moved 'Hummingbird' several times, always with some heavy barter and heavy banter for that matter but despite being a Wafi, a very good customer.

'Orla Korona' was a wooden yacht, built according to one story for a Polish Naval Officer. The intervening years had not been kind to it and around 1996 it was being used for drug smuggling. Being crewed by a team conspicuous by their 'townie' clothing and 'bubbled' by a rival drugs gang, Her Madge's Custom & Excise boarded her off Falmouth. The seasick crew asked to be put ashore (obviously not proper Wafis or they would have been enjoying the suffering) and pointed to the cargo down below, four tons of marijuana! The yacht was taken to Mylor, stripped to look for further loot, and then auctioned off by 'Customs'. The successful bidders were Brian and Sue, who became our customers and friends. Brian had been to see me in September 1997 with the specification for Orla Korona showing weight and dimensions that at the time were beyond our capabilities. However, I could offer transport because we were having Trailer 2 built and we would expect it to be in use by November. Brian and Sue's patience was sorely tried as deadlines for the move came and went with disappointing regularity, but eventually we could commit ourselves to the move.

Monday 4th May 1998 was a Bank Holiday. We were promised the trailer in full working order for Tuesday 5th. So, to allow a small margin for snagging jobs, surely no more after all this time, we agreed that we would travel to Falmouth to load early on the Wednesday afternoon. Loading was booked for two-thirty. We collected Trailer 2 late on the Tuesday afternoon, added all our straps, markers, blocks and all the other equipment that we would need. Retiring ready for an early start we were a little apprehensive as some of the support systems we had fitted to the trailer were new and untested. Starting up at 4a.m. on Wednesday, Bang! Lights blown! Despite my instructions that all the wiring had to be renewed, the trailer builders had used some of the old cables and had trapped a wire when welding a new part of the trailer. The fault took a lot of finding and we finally set off around 7a.m.

Stopping only to swap drivers and evacuate bladders we were blessed with clear roads. We were on the speed limiter all the way, arriving at Falmouth just as the boat was arriving, towed across from Mylor which was inaccessible to us. The boat went straight into the hoist area and was carried over the trailer immediately. We hardly had time to get the trailer set up when 'Orla Korona'

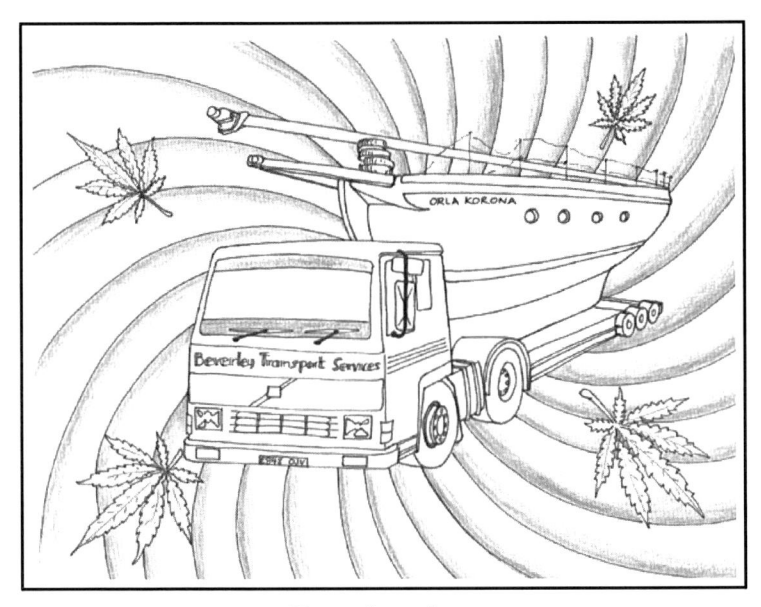

Drug bust boat

was lowered carefully into place.

Amazingly, everything worked well. Sue and Brian gave each other puzzled glances when I said to 'Q', "We should be OK when we get the hang of it". I referred to the support systems which were designed for the trailer and which were untried and as far as I am aware after all these years, unique. It must have sounded to Brian and Sue that this was our first job, and who can blame them.

Anyway, everything worked fine, so we strapped the boat down, showered and joined our customers in the clubhouse for food and refreshment. Our relief at the success of the loading was considerable. Neil slept on the comfortable bunk in the cab and I climbed into the boat and slept among the debris. No change there then 'Q'.

The journey back to Hull took almost two full days. The first police escort arrived promptly around six thirty on Thursday morning. They took us but a few miles and left us near Nanpean for the next team. Here we waited for hours until another escort arrived to take us across the old

China Clay workings to avoid a low bridge on the A30. These China Clay workings are now the site of the world class Eden Project and the low bridge has been by-passed. Thankfully, so have police escorts but more of that later. We were then abandoned near Launceston and waited many hours for the next escort. Several times whilst in Cornwall and Devon we were approached by people who knew the boat. 'Orla Korona' was infamous as the result of the drug-running stake-out and we had some odd reactions from people who were aware of her history. Rubbing salt into the wounds of our unreasonable delay, a police car arrived, the officer told us not to move as our boat was the subject of a police and customs prosecution and our lorry with its load would be impounded.

It's that blue and white sign again; 'Police Slow', as if we didn't know it! Despite our remonstrations, the promotion seeking plod would not even let us get into the lorry until he got clearance from Headquarters.

Friday morning and an early escort took us to the dual carriageway part of the A30. Then we were free to run on the M5, then stopped again to await another escort over the Avon Bridge. The duty officers were a bit over-zealous, convinced themselves that we were running at dimensions that had not been notified so took us to an industrial estate and did a quick measure. Realizing their mistake they laughed and left to find our way back to the M5. Thanks Plod! The final delay was waiting for Humberside Police to take us in to Hull Marina. Entering the marina at twenty past four, Darren, one of the hoist team muttered that he was supposed to finish at four! Welcome to Hull Marina!

For Sue and Brian this must have felt like the final insult after all the delays and problems. They spent considerable time, money and effort into restoring Orla Korona to her former glory. In the debris down below they found her original nameplate, 'Keflores' so the old name was adopted and often referred to as just 'Keffy'. Every aspect of the restoration was filmed and the much awaited launching was planned to coincide with another event, their wedding!

After the ceremony, wedding that is, they had a film show of the story which included part of the road journey. A great project and a privilege to be part of it.

Hidden away at a remote house in the beautiful Lincolnshire Wolds, a father and son team built a yacht from scratch. Their home is testament to genuine independence with a well for water, a generator for power and a workshop equipped for drilling, boring, turning and founding. Over a period of some years they had crafted, rather than assembled a long-keeled wooden yacht. Just about everything was made in their own workshop including paint. They wanted the yacht launched in Hull and one Sunday morning I visited the site to help plan the loading. During a tour of the premises I asked to use the loo and was directed upstairs. As the smallest room was dark, I tried the light and called out when it wouldn't work. Father instructed son to start the generator; a distant rumbling was heard coming from the workshop, the house shook, the contents of the kitchen rattled and as the power flowed around the house the loo light came on.

We had a cup of tea and discussed the loading, which was to take place two weeks later. There was a tree which would need chopping down, a prospect that filled the father and son with horror but on the day it proved necessary. There was a heatwave at the time and the boat was sprayed continuously to stop the timbers from drying out. By the time the loading day arrived the ground around the boat was saturated and the crane sank into the soil. But eventually, with the crane extracted from the soil and the offending tree cut down, the boat was successfully loaded. A remarkable pair of 'wafis'!

CHAPTER FOURTEEN

Tupperware Boxes & Gin Palaces

Those who sail by wind power regard themselves as purists and look down on motor powered recreation as second class and dismiss the craft as 'Gin Palaces' or in the case of fibreglass cruisers, 'Tupperware Boxes'. True, some of the owners can be snobs and often the boats are used as little more than floating caravans but the vast majority are just ordinary people messing about on the water. Their enthusiasm for boating has to be admired. They have been responsible for the revival, restoration and upgrading of many waterways including canals, rivers and docklands.

Our forebears showed stubborn, unbending determination when they built the canals, made rivers navigable and enabled sea-going vessels to reach the heart of the country. Towns like York, Norwich, Lancaster, Nottingham and Gloucester owe their growth and prosperity to trade and overcame physical, financial and bureaucratic obstacles to create the navigable waterways. The same indomitable spirit has been required for restoration projects in recent years. There is now a huge pool - poor pun - of boats, from the distinctive narrowboats of the canals, the broad beamed hire craft of the Thames and The Norfolk Broads to the estuarial and ocean going craft of the coasts. Most of these craft can be moved by road and many have covered more miles by road than in the water, and why not? I am continually amazed but gratified that, whatever the cause, our work keeps coming.

Often it is simply a case of the boat being purchased in one place for use in another. Sometimes the owners may choose to cruise on a different waterway for a season or even just for a holiday. In all cases we try to treat the boat as if it is our own and in many cases we have become good friends with the owners.

There are always exceptions of course. A lady rang me one morning and asked if I could take her Birchwood TS37 from a location in Yorkshire to a marina in the Midlands. She specified the following Thursday for the move. I said that we would be available and we agreed a price. I rang the boatyard to arrange loading and received the following blunt response.

"Don't even think about it, the owners are going through a very acrimonious divorce. The husband will be away on business next Thursday and she is trying to sell their boat behind his back. He warned us that this might happen!"

In the same area geographically and perhaps after the following conversation, in the same area 'matrimonially' was this telephone call one evening to a prospective customer. The lady of the house answered.

"Oh hello, sorry to bother you in an evening, is that Mrs. Wright?"

"Yes."

"Is Mr. Wright available please?"

"Who's calling?"

"It's Doug from Beverley Transport."

"What's it about?"

"It's about moving the boat."

"What Boat?"

End of conversation and possibly marriage.

Some of our customers will forsake their regular mooring for a holiday on a different waterway. Regular transfers are from Newark to the Broads, The Fens to the Thames and the waterways of the Ouse-Trent to the Thames, the Humber to the Broads and so on. Some are more ambitious and will go down to the south coast, go in at one marina, traverse the Channel and come home via a different one. Some may choose to go down by road and come back 'under their own steam' by water. Obviously we try to discourage that. Sometimes their plans are thwarted.

One year a couple with a beautifully maintained Fairline Mirage changed from Ely in Cambridgeshire to the Thames. They met up with other boaters from Ely and also from Buckden. All went well. The next year they decided to try the Norfolk Broads. Now fully retired they planned to spend the whole of the summer cruising. They were duly delivered to Brundall during the month of May. I noticed that they were well 'fendered up' with about about ten hung on each side!

"We'll be staying until October, but we'll give you plenty of notice when we're ready to come back"

"Help, we want to go home!"

This was their plaintive cry after but two weeks trying to avoid the advances of hire cruisers. They felt totally unsafe. Who can blame them? Many hire boaters are clueless when it comes to manoeuvring and mooring up. In some places, pressure for moorings is so great that boats are 'rafted' several together with crews climbing over adjacent boats to get ashore and worse, staggering and tripping over the same boats when returning from the pub! Within a few days we had rescued them and repatriated them to Ely.

Another Fenland Marina, Hartford, boasts one of the most ingenious boat lifting devices on the waterways. Consisting of a tractor, elongated frame plus cables and hydraulics, this machine can pick up and travel with boats up to about thirty feet in length. The process looks somewhat 'Heath Robinson' but with care and judicious packing with carpets, foam rubber and mattresses, boats are safely transferred. Thus, 'Lizzie B' has been a regular holidaymaker on the Thames, sometimes with a friend from nearby Earith who has a Dutch steel boat. One of the joys of boat transport has been the development of relationships with regular customers, both commercial and private.

A couple from Wakefield started with sports cruisers and yachts, moved up to bigger cruisers then back to yachts and in the process had their boats 'roaded' many times. We became good friends with them and enjoyed their hospitality and friendship on Solent cruises. We would take the boat to the coast, share part of their cruising time with them and bring the boat home when the cruise was completed. These times were very special. They were so keen on boating they even bought a marina and this of course brought us more work. Bob pushed a lot of jobs our way and was a beacon of good sense and generosity when the 'bank' hit us. His advice helped us formulate a plan to avoid receivership. He was a genuine Yorkshireman, a true friend and another good man taken before his time. Fancy That! (Not a smug remark, it was the name of his boat)

They say dog owners get to look like their pets and that the type of car you drive reflects your personality and so there is also a perceived correlation between the nature of the owner and his boat. Leaving out the Wafi syndrome for those propelled by wind, Jet Skis and small noisy sports cruisers may reflect snarling individuals with size complexes, people in a hurry, go-getters and the like. Sealine, Fairline and Princess cruisers tend to draw people of style and sportiness whilst Broom owners reflect solid judgement by people of substance. These are broad generalisations of course and no offence intended. They are all welcome as customers but some marques seem to attract controversy. Entering Hull Marina one day with a Tremlett cruiser, which I had collected from Southampton, a passing boat owner stopped in his tracks and gasped.

"Where did you bring that from, it belonged to a Glaswegian gangster!"

I didn't ask his involvement but it turned out that the first owner had been locked up. The boat, now but three years old had just a hundred and twenty four hours on the clock and had been 'purchased' if that is the right word by a Hull car dealer who had swapped it for a racing car. Two years later we moved it back down south and it had gained but three more working hours.

'Q' was on the M1 heading south when I took a call in the office. "Where are you going with my boat?" I didn't recognise the voice or the name and it turned out the boat had been sold on at least once and the caller claimed he was still the owner. The boat was delivered to Port Solent and presumably the ownership problem was resolved for we were paid and called upon to move it yet again twelve months later. This time we failed, for the boat had been so badly vandalised it was unfit for transport. Seemingly, one or more of the owners had started to re-furbish the vessel but got no further than the destructive phase.

Our next Tremlett was collected from Inverkip and delivered to Bell's at Brundall. The owner came as second man and because of delays waiting for police escorts we were incarcerated overnight at Southwaite Services on the M6. Neil's map of walkable pubs did not include this place and the weather was dreadful so no drink that night. The owner suffered considerably from alcohol deprivation but we made up for it the following night, Bonfire Night for what it is worth, parked by the railway line next to Bell Boats. There is a train through Brundall around five o clock every morning which can be heard leaving Norwich. The noise rises to a crescendo as it passes through Brundall at maximum speed and it can then be heard braking for Great Yarmouth. Some days it is merely a re-assuring 'constant,' leaving time for a bit more sleep but on this occasion it woke me with a jolt. I fell out of the top bunk, caught the door handle and fell all the way to the ground. This ignominious end to the trip must have been the curse of the Tremlett, nothing to do with the alcohol of course.

A trip to Scotland is always something to be cherished as readers will already know. So a Tremlett 42 with jet drives, from Chester to Lochgilphead was an opportunity not to be missed, or indeed given to 'Q'. The craft was delivered to an industrial estate near the town, where the owner, a confident, somewhat brash antipodean, would, in no time at all, according to him, restore it to full working order and performance. In submitting the bill I was invited to the owner's property which his wife ran as a Guest House on the side of the Crinan Canal.

Enjoying a cup of tea at the house I asked the lady if she was a boating fan, to which she rolled her eyes and commented somewhat testily, "All I said was, Bruce, it would be nice to have a boat to offer guests a little trip on the canal!" (On a jet driven power boat? Perhaps not).

Twelve months later I returned to the industrial estate to collect the Tremlett, not for launching as you might expect but to take it way up into the forest behind Kilmartin where restoration would proceed. Apparently there had been some disagreement between our customer and his landlord. Surely not! The boat seemed less seaworthy than when I had delivered it. This being February and me having come directly from Ireland and because Bruce had not booked a crane, I checked into their guest house for a couple of nights. On the Sunday I walked the Crinan Canal in bitterly cold windy weather feeling somewhat conspicuous by being dressed in

Bed, Breakfast and Boat

working clothes rather than walking gear. I need not have worried; coming the other way was a couple who had locked their keys in their car. They were dressed for an evening out, the lady complete with high heeled boots!

On Monday morning Bruce managed to get a crane to load us at the Industrial Estate then follow us to the forest location. We had a fall out over the poor site preparation, the bad ground conditions and the lack of supportive labour. Most of the work done to site the boat was done by the crane driver and me but eventually the boat was safely offloaded. Maybe it's still there, but in any case it's an unsatisfactory end to the story. We have had very few disagreements with customers but this one went wrong. I wonder if the Tremlett will or has ever taken the guest house customers on the Crinan Canal. As an odd sequel to the Tremlett syndrome we recently moved a 'forty-two' and the boat was exchanged for a van, an old Merc car and a bit of cash almost a match for the deal on the first one.

Newark Marina, on the River Trent is almost our second home. The strategic position part way to the Broads or part way to the Thames puts it on our route even when the work is not generated there. The generous management, James Wilkinson, family and staff, has allowed us to park there and use the facilities, a gesture that is much appreciated. Over the years they have introduced us to a lot of customers. We are particularly appreciative of the 'out of hours' unloading facility. If James is around and we need to be away early, he will come back in an evening to load or unload us. We have many friends at Newark and have had the privilege of moving them on several occasions. A Newark regular was successful with computers and was able to retire early to pursue, among other things, his love of boating. His Broom 38 probably covered more miles by road than by water, which is exactly how we think it should be! His home base was Newark but he has allowed us at various times to take him to the Broads, The Solent, Devon and Scotland. He would usually ride as "second man" and became quite conversant with the rules which governed our operation with abnormal loads. His interest in transport resulted in a well- received article in 'Motor Boats Monthly' which, although we were not mentioned by name, the photographs clearly identified us and gave us some good publicity. Thank you Stuart!

In years gone by, it was the role of the bus company or local council to control tree growth and for this purpose they often used a 'sawn off decker' with the indicator board showing 'Tree Lopping' or similar advice. No more. New buses are fitted with a vertical bar on the nearside front corner to deflect the branches and the only tree lopping is done by high loads. I have noticed some with bars on both front corners. They must go through thick woodlands I would assume. We have become a little

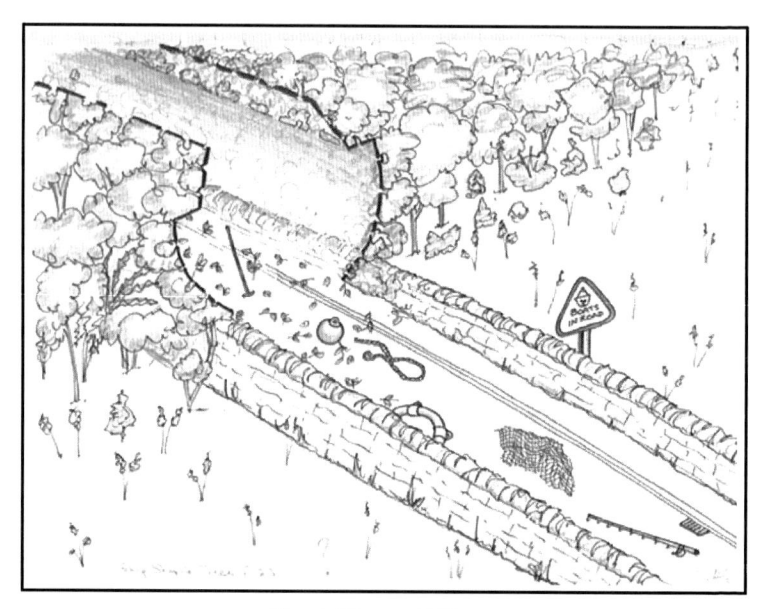

Boat Shaped Trees

hypersensitive about the risks and are declining to visit certain boatyards or marinas. Sometimes we put someone on the boat to push branches aside as the vehicle is driven slowly through the foliage. Sometimes though, heavy tree growth can be more demanding. One summer, 'Q' and I went to collect a superbly prepared cruiser from Fallwood Marina near Leeds to take to Pwllheli. There was an initial problem with craneage, the boat being steel and underneath power lines. However, despite the risks that this combination creates, the boat was loaded. Four men went on deck as we eased our way out of the marina and up the hill to the main road. Two had chain saws, the others hand saws. Painfully slowly we crept forward as the team cut away the offending branches. It took four and a half hours to move about half a mile and looking back the tunnel through the trees was now boat shaped.

Similar public service was carried out at Naburn some years ago. We were delivering a Princess 415 so Raymond sent a team to ride on the boat for the last couple of miles to clear the offending branches. The mess was considerable and held up a few inconsiderate motorists for a while. One big tree has prevented us getting in to Ripon Marina for it leans across the road and customers from here need to use other places if they wish to go by road. A formidable lady of advanced years and certainly of advanced boating experience hails from this marina.

It would, I think, be fair to say that boat handling is mainly a male activity. Usually, the man is at the helm, or steering wheel, doing the tricky, delicate, skilful bit whilst shouting at the crew, i.e. wife, partner or children, to get "fenders high, fenders low, grab the boat-hook, throw the rope, catch the rope, stand to attention, salute the captain," or other subservient acts. However, as in just about all of life's activities, man is put to shame by the opposite sex. More and more, it is becoming a woman's world! Anything he can do she can do better. So meet the intrepid Anne Walton.

Anne had been widowed but decided to carry on boating single-handed. She had a Nimbus 29 based at Ripon but wished to travel to, and on other waterways. She commissioned us to collect her from Newark at the appointed date and time and asked where we could deliver her to, in the Reading area? She had already been down the Ouse, out through the Humber, down the coast to Boston, back up the Humber, up the Trent to Nottingham and back down to Newark. She is a brave and resourceful lady to be sure. She declined our suggestion of Thames and Kennet for launching onto the Thames, opting instead for Better Boating at Caversham, run by good people to be sure but essentially an industrial yard with few facilities for a lady boater on her own. When we got there, Anne always rides shotgun, she was horrified to find that her boat had to be craned over two or three barges complete with welding sparks and smoke, which were being worked on, before being lowered onto her mooring. Things were basic to say the least.

"Why didn't you warn me?" she asked, as if it was my fault.

"I did," I replied somewhat timidly.

Despite this disappointing start to the cruise Anne navigated up the Thames and down into the tidal stretch. Late in the summer she prepared to return to the non-tidal part of the river and 'phoned to plan her re-patriation to Ripon via Newark. We agreed that Penton Hook Marina would be a suitable place for loading, but first Mother Nature intervened. It was a year of heavy flooding on the Thames and making progress upstream was difficult. To add to Anne's problems the Environment Agency had issued a warning not to try to 'lock upstream' in the river. But being mere men they could be ignored or over-ruled by our determined lady skipper. Being made of sterner stuff Anne duly braved and overcame the floodwaters to reach Penton Hook as planned.

When the boat was on the trailer, Anne carried out a visual inspection.

"There's some fishing line wrapped round the prop shaft, get some scissors and cut it off!"

Meekly obeying, I crawled under the back of the boat to cut the offending line only to discover that it was steel not plastic.

"Those are no good, why didn't you bring wire cutters?" she inquired.

"Cos I was told to use sci..."

Completing the sentence was pointless. Things are so obvious to women that argument is futile. We have had further commissions from Anne but after a visit to the Broads she announced she would not be using us any more as she was trading in her Nimbus for a Narrowboat. Despite this confident prediction we have been honoured to move Anne again, now in her eighties. This year she has travelled the Midlands and Northern canals in "Double U" her 32-foot canal boat and we collected her from Newark and delivered her to Naburn. Thank you Anne, may you cruise for many years to come!

'Doxy' is a name describing a 'hussey' or immoral woman. This accolade is totally inappropriate for Pat Tomlinson, wife of Chris, the owners of a steel cruiser now somewhere in the French canals. First we took them from Hull to Carlisle where 'Doxy' was re-furbished at their plant hire yard. Then we picked them up and delivered them to Amble and did the return trip for them to have the winter at home. Then back to Amble in the Spring. Later, having told us they wanted to go to the Norfolk Broads they were gently cruising through Newark when Neil rang them.

"Get a move on, we're off to Brundall tonight."

They were loaded and down to Brundall that evening. There must have been no Bingo on in Newark for 'Q' that night. Somehow without telling us they sneaked away to France. They toured the French canals for a couple of years then returned to England. Staying in Gweek Harbour they spent a winter replacing window frames and giving Doxy a general overhaul. In 2008 we took them along the south coast to Dover and away she went again to the Continent.

Neville Styles, computer expert, boat surveyor and owner of "Hot Property" a distinctive triple engined Sealine cruiser always makes clucking noises when he meets Neil. This originates from an incident on the A66 near Penrith shortly after Neil had left the services to head across the Pennines shortly after dawn. On the single track near Temple Sowerby the driver of an oncoming lorry failed to notice the wide load which was "Hot Property" because the driver had 'nodded off'. Neil swerved and at the last minute the oncoming driver looked up and swerved

Chicken Run

so cabs passed without touching but the trailers collided, or to be accurate, the trailer of the oncoming vehicle impacted on the boat. Nobody hurt fortunately but lots of feathers flying about. The trailer was loaded with live chickens and the impact caused considerable damage to the boat. The driver admitted falling asleep so our insurance was not used but we give thanks for safe passage and lack of injury. A few free eggs would have been handy too. Nev won't let 'Q' forget!

One delivery involved a burial at sea.

"I've bought a boat in Newark Marina and I want to scatter my father's ashes in the Irish Sea so will you take the boat to Brighton please?"

"Of course we will," I replied, and despite thinking that Brighton may not be the best route to the Irish Sea the Broom Crown was duly delivered to that marina. We never met the owner who was always on a train or on a station waiting for a train whenever we spoke, but he had left payment at Newark so we thought that was the end of it. However, some months later, calling whilst waiting for a train, he asked us to take it back to Newark. By then it was in Dover. The choice of Brighton for an expedition to the Irish Sea had seemed odd to say the least but you would have thought the best way would be to turn right (west) when leaving Brighton. Not so, our train riding, ashes scattering skipper. He had turned left and twice entered gunnery practice zones reserved for the Navy! He had been escorted into Dover Harbour by the Coastguard and been formally warned that the only way he could leave was by road. Where were Dad's ashes?

Talking of gunnery practice, did you know that Hitler had a boat like Britannia for State visits? A tender to this vessel had somehow arrived in Thorne. After the war, having been rejected for reparations by the Americans, it was accepted by the British. In the Nineteen Thirties, powered by one Mercedes engine the boat had been able to exceed twenty knots. The Brits replaced the petrol unit with two Leyland diesels and it struggled to achieve half this speed. Nevertheless, our optimistic customer would be restoring it to its former glory.

It was re-located to Penton Hook and later to Singapore.

Another southbound customer had a singularly rare reason for the move. He had a thirty foot cruiser at Naburn, near York and asked to be taken to the Thames.

"I'm registered blind and I've collided with many boats on the river so they won't let me out anymore. I'd like to go to the Thames where the river is wider so I'll have more chance of seeing the other boats before I run into them."

Ours is not to reason why, so the trip was duly planned. On the day in question, 'Q' loaded the boat on his own and I joined him at Naburn to share the driving and be "Second Man" on the next job. The boat was on the trailer and Neil was strapping down. The decks were cluttered with all manner of paraphernalia; bikes, buckets, plant pots, baths, fishing rods, fishing nets, barge poles, fenders, fuel canisters and gas bottles!

"Where's Mr. Newman?" I enquired of Neil.

"In his boat, thinks he's riding."

I climbed up the stern of the boat and shouted to the owner. Through the tangle of debris cluttering the deck appeared the heavily bespectacled owner, blinking at the daylight and squinting through thick lenses.

"How are you getting to Harleyford, you can't travel in the boat, it's not allowed."

Blinking and squinting even more desperately he argued, "I'll have to travel in the boat, I'm registered blind you know, I have no other way of getting there."

He looked so helpless that I reluctantly took pity on him. In no uncertain terms I said; "You stay below, lay on the bed and don't move. No lights. If we are stopped and you are discovered, we will claim you are a stowaway!"

We set off, 'Q' at the wheel until we stopped at Watford Gap to change over. Whilst checking round, I climbed up the back of the boat to see if our passenger was safe. I reaffirmed the order to stay out of sight and said we would be at our destination in a couple of hours. The A43, between the M1 and Oxford was still waiting to be made into dual carriageway. Even in the 1960s the trees had been cut back and an area reserved for the provision of another carriageway but nothing was done until the turn of the century. For much of the route the road was undulating, narrow and winding. Checking the rear view mirror whilst on a curve, I was alarmed to see the cabin lights through the windows of the boat. The first chance to stop to chastise the owner was Cherwell Valley Services. I climbed up the ladder and shouted.

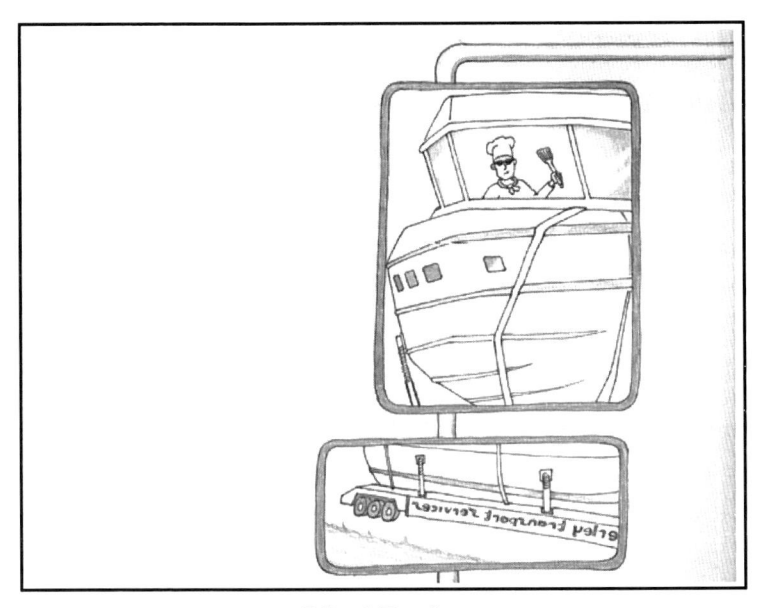

Blind Tasting

"Mr. Newman, are you there?"

The bottle bottom glasses sparkled through the gloom as he climbed up to the deck.

"I told you to stay out of sight, why are the lights on?"

"I was cooking a meal," he replied, seemingly oblivious to the legal risks to us and the safety risks to himself.

"Cooking?" I shouted, "whatever were you cooking for goodness sake?"

"Fish and chips."

So, registered blind, unable to get about on public transport, deported from one waterway to another for bumping other peoples' boats, permitted to ride on condition of secrecy and invisibility, he cooks fish and chips at fifty miles an hour on a poor road! Hmm.

A 'New Age' boater called Catherine came down from the upper reaches of the Trent to Newark. From there

New Age Cruising

she would be transported to Caversham. She was a live-aboard lady with a thirty-seven foot multi-coloured Broads Cruiser. The first notable point was that you could hardly see the boat for foliage. Along the roof were pots of various sizes and shapes containing shrubs, plants and flowers which shrouded much of the vessel. We had to move these items inside and into the front well area to allow safe transport. The lady was moving south to make her living on the Thames. She would be fabric weaving or other 'homespun' activities. I have a feeling that some of the plants would be used to supplement her income!

Another odd cargo came to light when Paul had loaded a cruiser to take to the Broads. The owner had watched Paul carefully load and make ready to drive away.

"Take care with my dogs," he shouted.

"What dogs?" said Paul

"My two dogs are on the boat, always go with us, have done for years."

"I'm sorry but we can't take dogs," Paul responded.

"It's OK," said the owner, "they're both in pots".

"But we can't take dogs!" said Paul more firmly, sensing trouble brewing.

"They'll be OK insisted the owner but don't tip them out or they'll get mixed up and we won't know who's who or which is which!"

Before Paul could reject him again, the boat owner explained, "They've been in the pots for years, dead and cremated, so you're carrying their ashes!" A much relieved Paul went about his business.

There are plenty of waterways in Ireland, both in the North and the Republic, *so there are!* In real life the Irish can make the jokes seem understated, *so they can!* Waterline Leisure, a customer near York asked us if we could put two twenty-four foot cruisers on one trailer to take to Ireland as their customer would only pay for one trip. We declined the opportunity but somehow knew that an Irishman would do it, for Irish hauliers are fearless. Some time later I was on the riverbank at York and asked if the sale had gone ahead and did anyone manage to get two boats on the same trailer. It had, and sure enough an Irish haulier had turned up to collect the two boats.

"Put one that way, one the other way and push them well up, I'll be putting a Combine on the back, *so I will.*"

He got away with it.

It was our privilege to take the first Azimut 39 to be imported to Northern Ireland. It went to Enniskillen from Swanwick in April 2000 on our Trailer One, *so it did.* Being for a new customer we did everything we could to get the job done right. The manager of the importing agents came as "Second Man" and we duly arrived at the marina. From the road to the water's edge was a zig-zag journey round immaculate lawns belonging to a golf course. The course owner watched every twist and turn to ensure that I didn't run over the grass, *so he did!* He reversed all the way along this tortuous route in his Beamer making my progress more difficult as he stayed just in front of the lorry. Anyway we completed the course to his satisfaction, *so we did.* Apparently, the marina had told our customer that they had a hoist which would lift his boat, but on arrival they bottled out and said the hoist was too small. There was impasse on the quayside, me demanding that they hire a crane, the boat owner saying he couldn't get one until the following week and the marina owner saying, "There'll be no crane over my grass. You'll have to use the slipway, *so you will!*"

There seemed to be little alternative but to comply. Their vehement insistence on 'slipping' the boat was matched by their persuasive hospitality and there can be few to match the Irish when it comes to conviviality. A very heavy night in the golf club bar left me staggering across the greens in the early hours to get some sleep and be ready for the launching ceremony. I'm not a great fan of Bushmills whiskey, the local hooch, but to refuse would have been unfriendly, *so it would!*

I was advised that the wheel bearings would be OK if they were cold, and the brakes would be OK once they had dried out after the 'slipping.' All the bulbs and lenses were removed and the rig was ready to reverse into the chilly waters of Lough Erne, *so it was!* Surprisingly, the lorry wouldn't just roll down the slipway, it had to be driven. The waters rose completely over the trailer wheels, then over the drive axle of the unit and were well up the front wheels, with the exhaust now bubbling fiercely through the water before the boat finally floated. It suddenly lurched upwards followed by all the timber packers, floorboards, carpets, straps and other loose items on the trailer, *so it did!* The crowd cheered and gratefully I engaged a forward gear to escape from the mud of the

Golfing Slipway

lough. That was easier said than done. The rear of the trailer was buried in the silt and the drive wheels were spinning. Eventually, the yard tractor gave assistance, *so it did,* and the lorry pulled clear. A helpful, black Labrador spent the rest of the morning swimming out to retrieve the timbers and other flotsam.

It took hours to clean the mud off the trailer and a charge for dredging would have been legitimate, *so it would.*

"We live to fight another day," is a phrase we often use and no more appropriate than on this occasion. The owner was pleased with the success of the job and had brought his chequebook. I had given him an invoice during the previous evening's festivities and left him to complete his details hoping he might add a bit for our substitute craneage. He freely handed over his payment. He was a car importer for a big Korean car franchise, *so he was,* but still essentially a family business. Some years later I was questioned at length by his cousin Gordon, the company accountant who had apparently found an anomaly in the records. The conversation was getting a bit complicated so I suggested that the boat owner could clarify matters. Unfortunately, he couldn't be questioned as he had passed away, *so he had.*

"Your invoice was for a delivery that it appears you never made," said Gordon accusingly.

"I assure you that we were worth every penny! After all this time what could you find wrong with the job?" I asked.

"We don't have a Rally Car, and *we never have had!"*

Another job where the customer had a distinctive accent started much nearer to home.

"Hi, My name is Cap'n Adam, just bought me a fine little cruiser from York, gonna head right down the Humber 'cross the North Sea and up the Rhine. Leastways, that was ma plan until ah hit the lock gates at Hull Marina."

The voice was a typical North American drawl and I had heard part of the story from Bob Bass at Hull Marina. He had indeed bought a small cruiser, a second-hand Birchwood 25 from Naburn, travelled down the Humber as far as Hull, hit the lock gates, damaging the gates and the boat, so he was holed up at a 'hotel' somewhere in town while the boat was repaired.

"I bin advised to go so far by road when the boat is repaired so ah need you guys to take it to Brightlingsea, then ahm gonna head right over the sea and way on up the Rhine"

He gave me the number of his alleged hotel and I was to phone him when the boat was ready to go.

"Just ask fer Cap'n Adam."

A couple of days later the marina advised that the repairs were complete and the boat could leave, subject to the owner paying his bill. I contacted Brightlingsea to book a crane.

"I understand you know Captain Adam," I said, using his confident assurance as an introduction.

"*Captain Adam*?" came the mocking, disbelieving reply.

"Oh yes, we know *Captain Adam,* he's a deck hand on an Anthracite boat that plies between here and the Ruhr, but he's no captain!"

I phoned his hotel to confirm arrangements.

"Hello, I believe you have a guest by the name of Captain Adam. Could I talk to him please?" Expecting there to be a delay while our man was located, I was surprised and a little suspicious when the Cap'n was immediately on the line.

"I'll have to leave at seven-thirty latest to get to Brightlingsea in time to catch the afternoon tide.

"I'll be there," said the Cap'n, "and I'll ride with you."

There was no sign of him the next morning so I called the number again and as before he was obviously next to the person who answered the phone.

"If we don't go now we'll miss the tide."

"You go right ahead buddy, I got me some business to sort out first so I'll grab a cab and follow you," ordered the Cap'n.

As I passed Grantham, he called again to advise that he was on his way. I arrived at Brightlingsea with about ten minutes to spare. I parked on the quayside, the strops were quickly slung around the boat and it was hoisted into the air. Normally the operator would have waited for payment before lifting but they knew 'Captain Adam' and were confident of being 'Brassed up.' As the boat was slung over the quayside a white taxi appeared and from it emerged the 'Captain' a man of considerable bulk who would have passed for a boxer. Care with descriptions is needed these days but he was of pure black African lineage rather than Afro-Caribbean but Anthropology is not my strong subject. I took a photograph with the boat in the air and the taxi in the foreground. I shook hands with the 'Captain', got paid and set off to the next job. I did not envy him the journey across the sea in such a small boat with an open cockpit.

Some twelve months later we had a visit from someone who knew a lot about 'Captain Adam' and wanted to know more. The visitor showed us his authority and drew breath to make an announcement.

"Our enquiries are on-going so I am not at liberty to divulge the nature of the activities we are investigating, but we know that whilst in the area the person who chose to be referred to as 'Captain Adam' bought a boat at Naburn, paid cash, damaged it, paid cash for the repairs at Hull Marina, bought some radio equipment, paid cash, had you to transport the boat to Brightlingsea and paid cash!"

He had a pretty thorough knowledge of the events of a year earlier so what was the purpose of the visit?

"He must have stayed with someone in Hull who not only provided him with accommodation but supplied large quantities of cash. We want to know who supplied the cash!"

The mysterious 'hotel' with the 'quick access' system must have been a safe house for the Captain. I keep notebooks forever but on this occasion I could not retrieve the number I had used to call him, which I thought would be the key to the enquiry. (It occurred to me that they probably got the number from Vodafone). I did manage to find the photograph of the boat and the taxi and offered to look for the negative.

"I'll take the print," said our inquisitor.

"We'll be able to blow it up to tell the time on the taxi driver's watch," he added somewhat haughtily. I wondered what was the point of that, for we knew it was

Turkish Demise

high tide at Brightlingsea at two-thirty, precisely as the taxi had arrived. Off he went with my picture and his secret. Some months later the case came to court. The intrepid 'Captain Adam' had been caught crossing the English Channel with twelve Turkish stowaways as his cargo! They must have been terrified.

CHAPTER FIFTEEN

Fishing Boats & Workboats

We have a high regard for fishermen and try to respond quickly and efficiently to their requests. There is a constantly changing pattern of fishing mainly due to the nonsensical Common Fisheries Policy, which has resulted in movements of boats of a certain size between the different fishing grounds. There are several reasons why moving fishing boats by road is good work. Firstly, the customers are generally straightforward. When they buy a boat they are often buying a quota or permit and want to be working as soon as possible. Therefore they are not so insistent on a return load price although we would always try to achieve one. After all, if we match up traffic to reduce empty running, everybody wins; the customers get a reduced charge but we can earn slightly more in total and there is less waste of resources. It is not always possible but we do try. Secondly, it is usually fairly easy to assess the overall travelling height of a fishing boat. Most have semi-displacement keels and therefore fit nice and snug, low down on the trailer. Taking the wheel-house height plus eighteen inches or so as a 'rule of thumb,' most vessels up to twelve metres in length can easily be prepared for the road. Removal of gantrys, aerials and radar is usually a straightforward exercise.

Compare this with the preparation of cruisers where the owners often add items to flybridges, arches etc., which can be difficult to remove and yachties who don't want the mast or wind generator removing! Fishing boats are less encumbered with things that can blow about in the wind, an important benefit when going down the road. Finally, fishing boats are tough, robust structures and can be strapped down quickly ready for transport without too much attention to the protection of glossy gel coats and shiny surfaces. That's not to say we don't take care, we certainly do, but however you look at it, fishing boats (and their owners) are less delicate than Wafis and less demanding than Tupperware mariners.

During the 90s there was no particular pattern to the movement of fishing boats just a general criss-crossing of the country; Hull to Largs, Whitby to Newcastle, Littlehampton to Hull, Dunvegan, Isle of Skye to Falmouth, Penryn to Burgh Castle, Bridlington to Gairloch, Hayling Island to Hemel Hempstead. Where? Hemel Hempstead with a fishing boat? Yes, an Aquabell 33 put into a caravan storage yard, but a stone's throw from the M1. There was little space available for the crane to set up and it arrived late in the afternoon with the driver exhaling strong aromatic fumes. The boat owner cum-would-be fisherman had not prepared the site, had no blocks, chocks or props to support the boat so 'borrowed' some of my timbers. The crane driver lowered the boat so quickly that when it touched the ground it lurched over and the strops went slack. He was unable to respond as he was somewhat worse for wear. With the owners help we levered the boat more or less upright and left my timbers propping it up. It was there for years, maybe still is.

Not only has the movement of fishing boats been a valuable source of work, it has brought us into contact with some fascinating characters. Take for example, Terry and Clint, father and son fishermen from Pwllheli who did a PX deal with a fisherman in Bridlington. The boat from Brid' was too big for roading so they would ride with me from Wales to Yorkshire and motor their new boat back by sea.

"Oooh, great truck this Doug," said Terry in a deep Welsh brogue as we stood sheltering from the wind at the front of the cab.

"What is she Doug, Scania?" he enquired, our heads almost level with the three letters of the badge on the radiator grille.

"Great trucks Scanias!"

"No, it's an M.A.N." I replied, "stands for Mean And Nasty," nodding towards the aforesaid badge.

"Ooh, great trucks aren't they!" my knowledgeable friend asserted.

"What engine's she got, Scania? Great trucks Scanias!"

"No, M.A.N. make their own and this has been a great truck too," I said quietly, patting Little Mandy on the nose and not wishing to get into a debate about the merits of different makes.

"The quality of our operation is in the trailer, it doesn't really matter what pulls it," I said, not wishing to offend Mandy or engage in Transport Café type, truck talk.

Boat loaded, strapped down and escort vehicle ready, father and son climbed into the cab. Clint took the passenger seat, leaving Dad to sit on the engine cover between us. The first few miles were quiet, all eyes on the road, the traffic, the escort vehicle and the physical obstacles on the route. Once past Bangor, now on reasonably adequate roads our fisherman resumed his friendly conversation.

"What do you do in your spare time Doug, watch telly I suppose?"

"Not much," I responded. "I don't get much spare time but I read quite a lot, enjoy rock'n'roll music and try to get to rock concerts whenever possible, generally to Sixties and Seventies' survivors like the Who, Paul McCartney, Bad Company, the Rolling Stones and so on."

He was impressed but countered with his own hall of

fame.

"Ooh, we've 'ad 'em all yurr," he proclaimed, "Dozey, Beeky, Lacy Paper, New Sneekers, Adam Firth, Willy Firy, Timmy Squeel, Oh Yes, we've 'ad 'em all yurr. Mind you, now the Butlins has gone we don't get them like we used to! So there it is then."

With few lapses in conversation our journey to Bridlington passed quickly and Terry and Clint, who had few words to add to his Dad's, paid their bill and boarded their new boat for the return journey. Despite the one-sided conversations I enjoyed their company and greatly respected them for the challenge of getting their new boat round the coast and back home to start work.

Another Terry, based in Leeds but buying up Bridlington has given us several good moves with his boats, some used for commercial fishing, others for private charters and diving. There is always a dispute over price and he swears he'll not use us again but I hope that he will. He has a friendly well- stocked pub in Bridlington too.

We received a boost to our association with fishermen and fishing ports in recent years with a journey, which nearly foundered. Just before Christmas 2002 I received a call from a young man who had bought a boat at North Shields, a Kingfisher 33, which 'Q' had brought up, brand new in 1997, from the factory in Cornwall. Tristan wanted it taking to Craobhaven near Oban. Eager to start fishing the buyer wanted to go before the holiday break but there was insufficient time. So, as the world struggled back to work early in the New Year I went to Royal Quays to load the boat and yes, embark on another trip to Scotland.

So, with Tristan aboard we set off in very cold conditions and increasing amounts of snow. We got on well, with Tristan outlining his plans to start fishing off the Ardnamurchan Peninsula and we talked about the area and the journey ahead. Suddenly, as we crossed the Pennines on the A69 the penny dropped. I had measured the travelling height at sixteen-foot three and there was a bridge at Tarbet on our route, which was sixteen-foot nothing! I had completely overlooked this when loading, how unprofessional! At our first break I discussed the possible options with Scottish police who it has to be said are generally very helpful with Abnormal Loads. All other routes were rejected either for lack of craneage or even lower bridges.

The name 'Tarbet' or Tarbert' is Viking for a place where their boats could be dragged from one stretch of water to another. It looked as though it might have to be tried with our fishing boat! Arriving at the booth on the Erskine Bridge, the toll collector chuckled at the name.

"We've just had an American tourist go through here asking for directions to Ten En Ay. I couldna recognise the place. He said it was an old religious centre where Christianity had started or something. He pointed to it on the map. Iona!"

The name of the famous Scottish island and by coincidence, our boat!

We were to meet our Police escort at Tarbet, by Loch Lomond and if we couldn't get under the bridge, the Viking method might be an option!

The Abnormal Load Officer at Strathclyde Police was a positive thinking individual and offered the notion that they had "scalloped the road a wee bit" so we might get through. He'd send an escort at first light the next day and they would take us to the bridge and hopefully beyond. His words of encouragement, with apologies to speakers of the Scottish dialect, went thus; "We'll close the road and take ye ta tha bredge; if ye canna get under we'll ha ta put ye in the car park while ye work out a solution. Mind ye, eff ya hett tha bredge they'll shut the railway and a man from Hornby will bring ye a great beg bell."

So, on day one, we reached Tarbet and parked

opposite the Tarbet Hotel, which was closed. There was a pull-in, which had previously been a filling station, long since closed and subsequently commandeered for overnight parking for HGVs. (It is national policy not to have these nasty beasts parked anywhere civilized, so this little oasis of relative security was soon to be blocked off by the authorities using huge boulders. The wide load waiting area was transferred to Strathgowan lay-by, a mile out of the village.) On this occasion we were able to park in the village but Tristan didn't want to sleep in the lorry or his fishing boat. Although Little Mandy had a heater it would be a long cold miserable night. We sought accommodation but there was nowhere open in Tarbet. As we sat somewhat disconsolately, the council gritter/snowplough pulled up.

Now having a boat on a lorry is like walking a dog, everyone wants to know you. Walk round anywhere on your own you must be up to no good, someone to avoid, possibly a pervert. But if you have a dog you must be a good person so you get a friendly approach; "Ooh, isn't he/she lovely, how old is he/she etc. etc.

Likewise, having a boat on a lorry usually attracts friendly comments such as "She's a classic isn't she, It's a Dunkirk veteran isn't it, she's been around the world, where's that from or where's it going?" So the ploughman admired the boat, had a cup of tea with us and then offered us a lift to Arrochar, the next village where there would be accommodation. Gratefully, we squeezed into his cab and received a demonstration of a high-tech gritting process. Apparently a satellite receives the temperature information from the road ahead and then instructs the gritter when to grit and how much to dispense. Impressive!

We were safely delivered to Arrochar, booked in at a friendly B & B and dined at the adjacent restaurant. There was also a bar next door and a very convivial evening followed. Tristan introduced me to an Islay malt whisky called Bunnahabhain, pronounced 'Boonaharven'. Quite how the late Moonwalking, 'Bad' singer became involved I have no idea but Michael Jackson describes this malt as "Rich, amber. Thick, honey, fruitcake, gingerbread."

All I know is that it is a delightful brew, very smooth and according to Tristan, best taken with a 'wee dash of cold water."

Under different circumstances the accommodation would have been idyllic for we were given a small outhouse on the shore of Loch Long. Certainly, this would be a picturesque scene, but in early January, bitterly cold, outside too.

Answering the call of nature in the 'wee small hours' (pun?), I was rudely brought back to reality. Had I measured the height of the boat correctly, was it really sixteen-foot three? Could it actually be more or perhaps it could be less? No more sleep, just constant nagging anxiety about the potential for failure in the day to come.

At last, time for breakfast and a taxi back to Tarbet. The parking area now had three mobile homes parked behind our boat all waiting to join our convoy. I climbed to the top of the boat and again carefully measured to the highest point.

"Oh what joy, Sixteen Foot One!"

The euphoria was short-lived when returning to ground level I noticed the dreaded bulge in the tyre. We had a puncture, which had reduced the height by the two inches I thought we had 'gained'. Worse still, the police escort was on its way and although I carried a spare wheel, I did not have a jack.

Undoing and tightening wheel nuts is tiring, or tyring, get it? at the best of times but here, now with the clock ticking and the job looking dodgy, already it was a frantic, exhausting activity. The absence of the jack was remedied with the use of the air suspension Raise/Lower facility, fairly crude but it worked. Just as the Police arrived I was tightening the nuts on the newly fitted wheel.

Being aware of our predicament with regard to the height, they proposed to take us to the bridge alone leaving the caravans in the parking area. If we got through they would come back for the caravans; if we failed they would park us up at a restaurant near the bridge while we sought a solution. (I suspect that given similar circumstances, most English Police would have refused to attempt this procedure and would have just left us. It is worth noting again that Strathclyde police, particularly those based at Lochgilphead have over the years provided a thoroughly professional but friendly and helpful escort service).

Tristan rode on the boat in order to watch the clearance under the bridge. The police closed the road, we inched our way forward and I could see they were taking photographs. Tristan gave the thumbs up and we proceeded to another lay-by while the police went back for the mobile homes. Tristan climbed down, I nipped up the wheel nuts on the newly fitted wheel and we both felt very relieved for the clearance was a mere centimetre!

The convoy of two police cars, one boat and three mobile homes made its way through Argyll along the shores of Loch Long, over the 'Rest and Be Thankful' mountain pass and along the shores of Loch Fyne to Inveraray. With narrow streets and parked vehicles there was some delay here and two caravans left us for separate destinations. By Lochgilphead there was only the boat and the police. We were left here for a while as these officers had to attend a funeral so I checked the wheel nuts again. Eventually, a sergeant arrived to take us the rest of the way. As light was fading we arrived at Craobhaven, much relieved and sensing the anxiety was nearly over. We thanked the officer and he returned to Lochgilphead while we unstrapped the boat and prepared for lift off and launching. But Professor Sodd had another trick up his sleeve!

A Tight Squeeze

As the hoist started to move and make its way to pick up the boat it suddenly lurched to one side with a collapsed wheel bearing. Luckily, Ardfern, a nearby marina where we were fairly well known had a working hoist and we could go round there. The police escort car couldn't be reached by radio but mercifully the controller allowed us to move in the company of any vehicle with flashing lights which we commandeered from Craobh'. It was fully dark as we reached Ardfern and the hoist operator 'China' calmly removed 'Iona' and launched her.

Thus, this epic journey came to an end but gave rise to many more. Several weeks later, a mysterious parcel arrived, quite heavy and extremely well wrapped. After tearing through several layers of packaging and insulation there was a glorious bottle of Bunnahabhain. Also in the package were several photographs of 'Iona' squeezing under the bridge at Tarbet. The police had taken photographs with Tristan's cameras when he had been on top of the boat and I had thought they were just collecting evidence! I telephoned Tristan to thank him for the contents of the parcel.

"Oh, that's OK," he said.

"We thought you had done a good job. Dad's put you on his website!"

Dad is David Cochrane, whose website "Find a Fishing Boat .com" has become the 'bible' for the trading of fishing boats and equipment. This site has been a good source of work and we keep up the entry with a banner and link to our own website.

There are certain boats that for whatever reason, seem to move more miles by road than they do by water. This of course is to be encouraged as it generates work for us but the benefits can be multiple. For example, in 2005, 'Q' took 'Lady Frances' a fairly heavy twelve metre fishing boat from Royal Quays to Whitehaven but she couldn't settle. In 2007 she came back to the North Sea but further south, to Felixstowe Ferry, a delightful little boatyard just outside Felixstowe itself at the mouth of the River Deben. The new owner Craig came as "Second Man" for this journey and we arrived at the boatyard to commence off-loading. Heath Robinson had set up their equipment. They had a hoist but that could only reach about halfway along the boat, so they added muscle with an excavator bucket and yet more muscle with a forklift. Despite their enthusiasm and determination the "Lady Frances" would not budge. Eventually, with judicious lowering of the trailer and determined heaving by all parties the boat seemed to come clear.

"Go! Go! Go!" came the shout, and rather slowly and somewhat jerkily I moved away. All seemed well as I walked back to sort out the trailer. Then I noticed the damage. All the rubber pads had been ripped off the cross members and were neatly laid on the floor. Nobody had seen it happen or if they did they had kept quiet. I am prone to shoot from the hip and I let rip with some verbal abuse but to their credit they got stuck in and realigned the pads nearly as good as new. They were forgiven and good relations were restored. From that encounter we have had several jobs, all of them satisfactory. A bonus when 'overnighting' here is the clubhouse. They have showers, a well-stocked bar, sometimes do food and have a delightful collection of signed Giles cartoons featuring sailors and sailing. A genius of humour for sure.

Later that month, James White, one of the Felixstowe Ferry fishermen had a deal arranged with a fisherman at Brixham. We set off with his old boat to do the exchange at Darthaven, a marina on the Kingswear side of the Dart, truly one of the most beautiful settings in the British Isles. Going down, his boat was only twenty-five foot by ten but his new one "Krystal Kay" was thirty-five by twelve and would require a "Second Man", James, and an escort out of Darthaven. One September afternoon we arrived in Darthaven and were prepared to stay the night but no sooner had we booked in with the lifting crew than Brian Fenton (the top abloads escort man in the South West) turned up ready to take us out. We hadn't anticipated his early arrival and I was looking forward to a night exploring Dartmouth but the hoist team readily obliged and we were turned round in just over an hour. Brian took us to the dual carriageway on the outskirts of Torquay and from there we were free to run alone. We had just enough time to reach Gordano Services near Bristol and park near the mound at the rear of the site. James' sad expression soon lifted as we escaped from the MSA and I led him over the mound and across the field to the village for a couple of pints and a proper meal in very hospitable surroundings. (See 'Q's MSA refuges in Chapter Eight).

James was very obliging or was it self-preservation; we took the boat for lift-off at Ipswich Haven to avoid the nerve jangling lift at Felixstowe Ferry.

Fast forward to February 2010 and James has moved up to a brand new Kingfisher 33, possibly the last one out of the factory in Cornwall and loaded by the most uncooperative boat builder I have ever come across. The wheelhouse was separate but couldn't be put inside the hull because the hoist wouldn't lift high enough. The owner, James would have to pay if a crane had to be hired. A difficult load and a very difficult loader. Having said that, it made the equipment at Felixstowe Ferry look positively sophisticated in comparison. The wheelhouse, which we had perched on the swan neck of the trailer, was easy meat for the excavator bucket and the 'halfway' hoist took most of the weight of the hull. It just needed a little assistance from the excavator bucket but the hull had no lifting points. Where there's a will, there's a way, they say and the boat was duly off-loaded. 'Krystal Kay' previously of Darthaven and now late of Felixstowe Ferry was relocated to East Llanion in Milford Haven to be off-loaded by our good friend Vance. Sadly, despite the enthusiasm and ingenuity of the boys at Felixstowe Ferry, a crane had to be hired for the send-off.

In the bleak mid-winter, 'Q' and I loaded the 'Sallian' at Fleetwood for delivery to Felixstowe Ferry. Snow was disrupting traffic all the way to Suffolk and Operation Stack was implemented as Felixstowe port was closed. We managed to sneak into Ipswich Yacht Haven and discussed possibilities with the buyer who happened to have a crane company operating on the dock. Next morning, the snow was thick and fresh as we skidded into Felixstowe Ferry. It was so cold the 'legs' on the crane froze up but eventually the boat was lifted and we skidded back to civilization.

Sadly, not all our stories involving fishermen have

happy endings. In June, 2006, Neil took 'Pamela S' from Grimsby to Dale Sailing at Neyland in Milford Haven. Doug Hook accepted the boat and was to work 'Pamela S' with his brother in law. On their first trip, whilst familiarising themselves with the vessel, it simply sank! The two were cast into the sea, unable to grab life rafts or jackets. Doug held his brother in law afloat for seven hours until they were both washed ashore. Doug was found unconscious and survived but sadly his companion perished. Doug's wife phoned to tell me the sad news and I phoned 'Q' as it was he who had met them when delivering the boat. Coincidentally, at that very moment he was loading a damaged fishing boat at Itchen Marine in Southampton under the instructions of the Marine Accident Investigation Board inspector. The boat was to go to Cranfield College to be used for rescue training. As 'Q' recounted the story, the inspector told him he was going to Milford Haven to examine the wreck of the boat! But the story does not end there. Less than two months later Doug found a replacement, in Kinlochbervie, North West Scotland. Knowing how Scotland is wasted on 'Q', I took it upon myself to do the job. With some juggling I managed to work in a northbound load to help with costs. A long keeled yacht was loaded at the Elephant Boatyard at Swanwick for delivery to the Old Rothesay Dock, now called Clydebank Marina. This left Friday clear for the journey to Kinlochbervie to await the crane on Saturday.

The route from Inverness is one of the very best scenic journeys across some of the remotest parts of Britain and along some of the most primitive roads too! The landscape here is made up of some of the oldest rocks in Europe, some 3,400 million years old would you believe and the area has undergone multiple convulsions and upheavals ever since. Although it was still summer time and the weather very pleasant I decided to get 'digs' in order to catch up with washing, showers etc.

I also wanted to explore. I mentioned my interest in Geology to the fisherman, the vendor of the boat and he straight away reeled off the names and locations of famous geological features. To add to my fulfilment of the weekend he even lent me his van. "Northern Lights" was duly loaded on the Saturday morning and I spent the rest of the time exploring. Work cannot get better than this. It took nearly two days to reach East Llanion to meet up with Doug, his wife and their brand new baby. We spent a very sociable evening around Milford Haven drinking in good company and reflecting one life lost and a new one begun.

"How can you go back to sea after the loss of your brother in such circumstances?"

"It's in the blood," said Doug. His wife smiled, shrugged, and hugged the baby.

Hopefully, I thought and probably expressed, "Northern Lights" will prove to be a better boat than "Pamela S".

Vance, from East Llanion Marine unloaded the boat next morning and re-loaded a yacht for Essex. Overall, this was good matching of loads with one going two-thirds of the way up to Kinlochbervie and another paying more than half way back from Wales. It was a decent run with many side benefits.

Whilst full of praise for the men who brave the hazards of the sea to make a living, it's true to say that the industry attracts its fair share of characters and indeed some rogues, and we've met some of them. It's human nature that where a government, be it local, national or continental tries to organise men or industries through rules and restrictions, those very men and industries will find ways to thwart them. And so, in the 90s, when the CFP contrived to deprive fishermen and their boats of their waters, a range of responses kept the boats afloat and the men at work.

Over-capacity, over-fishing and government interference brought about a process that would theoretically solve some of the problems; *de-commissioning.*

In some ports, for example Girvan, you can find a number of vessels that look as though they have been rammed against the harbour wall, being blunt rather than having a sharply pointed prow. These craft had fallen foul of the new rules by being half a metre too long for the new specified dimensions and the owners would be offered a significant payment to decommission them. So, the owners took the money, chopped half a metre off the front of the boat and put the boat back to work! One of our customers in Bridlington took the money, had the boat cut in two, had a section cut out and the two sections stitched back together. This was common practice, with some re-builds unfortunately being unsafe. A wooden coble, de-commissioned out of Scarborough was taken to a pub at Flamborough Head and burnt on Bonfire Night. A sad end.

The authorities eventually wised up to the various schemes that the fishermen had used to circumvent the regulations and in 2009 de-commissioning was carried out in a more ruthless way. The boats were to be destroyed completely and the destruction photographed by DEFRA staff. Thus we took some ten boats from the North East coast - Amble, North Shields, Hartlepool, and Grimsby - to 're-cycling centres', otherwise referred to as scrapyards. We got a big shock on our first and last visits. When we are loading, the equipment used, whether it be a crane or a hoist, enables the boat to be lowered safely onto the trailer. There must be no damage, not even superficially. Equally, when unloading, the converse is essential.

Imagine the shock when Neil arrived at the scrapyard to be told; "Park over there pal, we'll push the boat off."

"Oh no you ******* won't," said Neil, "you'll lift

Defra Destruction

it off properly!"

After a short impasse, with the DEFRA camera ready to roll, and Neil ready to take the boat back from whence it came, the scrapyard staff devised a method. Not ideal, not Health and Safety compliant, but a method.

One mechanical grab would clamp its vicious jaw onto the wheelhouse and the other would grip the stern. Lifting together, the pair would raise the boat in the air, and the vehicle would then pull forward out of the way. Or not.

The grabs lifted unevenly and the wheelhouse collapsed, letting the boat drop back onto the trailer. Ten tons of boat, dropping merely a foot, has quite an impact and some damage occurred to the supports. Chains were added to the jaws of the grab and slowly the boat was raised up, enabling a much-relieved Neil to draw forwards. Subsequent visits were equally worrying and we incurred damage to both trailers. The scrapyard upped its game by utilising three grabs to lift, an exercise in co-ordination and some considerable stretching of nerves.

Our last boat was taken to a different scrapyard where the owner had negotiated a better deal, or so he thought. Unfortunately, this yard was unaware of the finesse required for off-loading and only had two grabs available. The boat was raised slightly but was too heavy and it dropped violently back onto the trailer. Paul and I were thinking the worst, that the trailer would not be usable again. It was pushed into the ground and looked twisted and broken. Eventually, another crane was brought from another yard and the boat was removed. We limped back to Hull and set about sorting out the necessary repairs. It turned out that the owner had been a bit naughty. The deal from DEFRA was; scrap the boat and claim the agreed de-commissioning grant. The scrapyard would then destroy the boat, and charge for that service but pay for any scrap 'weighed in'. Thus, the owner of a fibreglass vessel would get his 'comp' plus maybe a bit for the engine, winch etc. but then have to pay for disposal of the GRP. The owner of a steel boat would get his DEFRA money plus quite a lot more for the 'weighed-in' metal.

Our boy with the last boat thought he'd hit the jackpot with the new scrapyard, having negotiated a higher rate per ton for the 'weigh-in'. True enough, we had felt a heavy boat behind us as we drove from the Royal Quays to the scrapyard near Walker. We struggled to get any help from the boat owner in the cost of repairs. Phone calls, e-mails, messages totally blanked until... it transpired that much of the weight for which he had been handsomely rewarded was not in fact metal, but was around twelve tons of concrete ballast! I think our subsequent payment was the result of the scrapyard seeking retribution, bringing about a certain amount of contrition.

Allied to work with fishermen, there are several other groups who use boats to earn a living and sometimes have the need for road transport. Harbour authorities, Coastguards, Police, Surveyors and other offshore industries all use boats that can be moved by road. The 'in' game recently has been wind farm construction and their support vessels need to be moved around sometimes at short notice. The movements are not on such a personal basis as with fishermen, but still, it is good work.

CHAPTER SIXTEEN
Police & Pretend Police

Abnormal loads, whether they be high, wide, long or heavy must be made conspicuous by markers and flashing lights. These markers must be of a defined size, colour and pattern. Where these loads exceed certain dimensions, the police forces along the route of the journey have to be informed. Various criteria have to be specified and the police then consider if the journey can be approved. The "Abnormal Load Notification" form must be submitted by fax or the modern medium, e-mail, giving two clear working days' notice. Some Forces will always reply, some will occasionally reply and some never reply. Abnormal loads officers may be civilian or serving police officers. Some work regular hours and are available to give guidance to hauliers. Some spend more time away on courses than they do in their own office. (One Force has an answer machine message on the Abnormal Load Officer's landline which has not been changed for over six months and it goes like this; "This is the voicemail for 'George Dixon' who deals with Abnormal Loads and Burglar Alarms and is on Annual leave until 28th August". As today is 10th February it does show that police get proper holidays).

The Abloads Officer may if necessary suggest a different route, a restricted time, or an escort vehicle to accompany the load for part of or all of the journey. In most cases in England the escorting will now be done by a private or self escort but not long ago the police did all the escorting themselves. Their services were generally free but only available when conditions released them from other tasks. Delays waiting for police escorts would often be for several hours and could even go beyond a day.

There used to be a saying in general use about the Police; "If you love animals join the mounted police or become a dog handler. If you like water, join the river police. If you hate people join the Traffic Police!" This, in our experience is an unjust comment for there are good and bad in all groups of people but overall we were dealt with in a very professional manner by the teams who were sent to escort us.

Some, particularly the motorcycle cops, were a bit over the top at times. Travelling along the M4 in Gwent one day, 'Q' and I were being escorted by two motorcyclists who thought they belonged to the California Highway Patrol or 'CHIPS' as the television series called them. Complete with the obligatory 'shades' they took it in turns to lead us or follow, weaving between lanes cutting up other vehicles in dramatic fashion. At one point they straddled the lorry and each one shouted up to us, asking about the height of the boat we were carrying. They made out that the scaffolding in one of the tunnels up ahead would be a problem. They stopped us on a slip road, had a chat between themselves, then ushered us away and through the tunnel.

Motorcycle escort riders seem to get bored very easily. In Bradford one Saturday, we were under escort with a large yacht heading towards Bingley. Ahead, crossing the road was a little old lady with a shopping trolley. She had reached the middle having crossed our side of the road and was looking towards on-coming traffic. One of our brave outriders drove up behind her and when he got close, set off his siren. She jumped out of her skin and looked terrified but our hero just drove on. Some retribution occurred near the end of the journey as we followed some country lanes. At a humped back bridge,

Brave Escort Rider

our hero zoomed over the top and sped away into the distance. We turned left before the bridge, drove behind some buildings and met up with the crane. Evel Knievel took quite some time to realise his mistake and even longer to find us. His mate gave him some well-deserved abuse when he finally arrived.

With flashing lights, beacons, patterned markers and police vehicles in attendance, wide loads are still invisible to the average motorist! Once the patrol car is out of sight, the purpose of the escort is lost on the viewer and he carries on regardless. On an Essex road one day, 'Q' was following a police escort along roads where on-coming traffic had to keep tight in to the left hand side. Progress was slow and tedious and certainly frustrating for the following vehicles. It has always been our policy, wherever possible, to pull in regularly to allow the road to clear of delayed vehicles. I believe this is 'best practice' and is merely common courtesy. Where confronted with aggression by angry motorists, I invite them to consider that they have not been delayed but have been included in a very important procession. Sometimes the Police will do this, sometimes not. On this particular day, impatience gave way to bravado and one by one several cars managed to squeeze past the boat only to find 'Plod' at the front! He stopped the convoy, parked the offenders at the side of the road and told them he would be back to book them after the completion of his escort duties. Nice one!

I think it was the North Wales Police who started the privatization of escorts and it became almost a frenzy. When a proposed route was notified, the response was to have an escort here - say on a narrow bit of road, there - say through some roadworks, and everywhere there could be a potential hazard. It was particularly frustrating in that all of a sudden, stretches of road which had been deemed to be safe enough when the police were responsible for escorting, now required an escort because the police were not involved. This occurred in several counties as the privatisation spread. All in all though, whilst private escorts have to be paid for, they do turn up when booked whereas police, although they normally did not charge, only turned up when they had no other priorities. So, in general the privatisation of escorting has been a beneficial change, freeing the police to pursue other tasks and generating work for hauliers and escort businesses.

As is often the case, customers know best, telling us, "It won't need an escort," because last time it was moved it didn't need one. The decision is not ours, or theirs, but in some places we will insist on an escort even if the police have not ordered it. For example, leaving Harleyford Marina, a beautiful spot on the Thames, there is a section of the A4155, a distance of about one and a half miles into Marlow, where space is minimal, even for fairly small boats. There always seems to be a bus or oncoming lorry to intimidate us, so the use of an escort would seem wise.

The requirements for escorting are based on a Code of Practice rather than a rigid rule book or law and a network of registered providers cover most of the country.

Simon Hands, a man with considerable marine experience set up Convoi Exceptionnel Ltd. Covering all aspects of planning, notifying and escorting of abnormal loads, they provide a national and international service. They can even negotiate permit and Pilot car rules in the Republic of Ireland! We do not have enough escort work to justify operating our own vehicle but we have established relationships in the areas where we need escort cover. In our local area, a big centre of caravan and cabin production, we can call on the caravan transporters or Stav from Wide Load Escorts Ltd. The Scottish Borders are covered by Lyne Caravan Transport or Andy Brown. Further north John Shepherd, Rayliable Transport or Alistair Cameron help us when we are in their region.

In North Wales, Mike from Glanaber is our first call. In South Wales John Kilcoyne has had a more or less seamless transfer from escorting as a policeman to private escorting as AAA abnormal load escorts. In adjacent counties Ian Brooks Road Pilots provide a very professional service.

In the West Country our good friend Brian Fenton is a gentleman in the full sense of the word, with an impeccable pedigree for escorting boats. He used to move boats himself with some very distinctive, even unique vehicles. Now well past retirement age, Brian gives a friendly, thoroughly efficient escort service.

In Hampshire, there couldn't be a better lineage for moving abnormal loads than that of Chris Hill, from the famous Hills of Botley family, whose distinctive and much improvised heavy haulage vehicles span more than a lifetime. Clarks Transport, caravan and boat hauliers in their own right also give an excellent service in this area.

Further east, Sussex Police have a strict but

consistent policy for abnormal loads. All notifications receive a reply and a permit defining how the move shall be carried out. Terry Ollerton, our friendly competitor from Shoreline Yacht Transport, Mark Paine of Southern Caravan Services and Malcolm Webb of Plant Hire, all supplement their incomes with escort services.

CPL covers Kent and John Reynolds the area west of London. Debbage Yachting help us in Essex and Suffolk and we look to Kingsley Farrington our colleague in The Broads for cover in that area. Malcolm Elvy and Pete Downs, both long established boat hauliers have escort vehicles for hire as well as covering their own escorting.

So privatisation of escorting has generally been of benefit to abnormal load hauliers and we welcome this situation. Of negative impact, however, is the increasing number of 'No Go' times for abnormal load movements. Certainly, rush hour limitations in urban areas make sense but there are some extensive rural roads, even motorways, apparently even whole counties, where abnormal loads may not move between 07.00 and 10.00am. or 4.30 and 6.30pm. In some areas it's getting hard to do a decent day's work. It's such a shame that restrictive practices impede normal progress.

CHAPTER SEVENTEEN
Marinas & Boatyards

The places we visit in our everyday activities might have been plucked from holiday brochures.

"Come Sailing on Windermere", "Cruise the River Thames" or "Hire a Boat on the Norfolk Broads", are typical slogans advertising the virtues of the Inland Waterways of England. Add the River Severn, River Trent, several River Ouses, plus hundreds of miles of canals and the enormous potential for boating activities becomes apparent. Scotland has several important canals and of course the spectacular Loch Lomond to attract the boating community and Ireland has many navigable rivers, canals and lakes or 'loughs'.

The landscapes within Britain are complemented by the coastline with its enormous variety of scale and relief. The southeast is generally lower and straighter than the rugged north and west. Headlands, bays, coves, estuaries and cliffs make the contact between land and sea and generate a range of maritime activities.

The coast and the inland waterways between them provide us with a large number of locations for the start and finish of our journeys. The businesses at these points of contact are the boatyards and marinas with which we share customers. Thus, we get to visit interesting places, meet nice people and generally get well treated. It's comforting to know that at journey's end there will be safe parking, shower and toilet facilities, and often even a bar and restaurant. And this is supposed to be work!

We try to book our visits well in advance and keep in

touch if we are delayed or our plans are changed. We understand that at certain times the yard staff are very busy; for example bringing boats onto hard standing at the end of the season and launching them at the start of the next season. In return we hope for cooperation and flexibility when we have travelled perhaps three hundred miles to reach the site and may have been delayed by traffic conditions. Most of these places are friendly, hospitable and accommodating. Obviously, some are visited more frequently than others, so we have different relationships. There are very few where we are not welcome and very few that we are not keen to visit. Oh, what a contrast with general haulage and supermarket work!

Some places are particularly noteworthy.

Hull Marina has been our home for over twenty years and was the starting point for our early efforts in boat transport. The marina was established in the 1980s by the Hull City Council, 're-cycling' a disused commercial dock. Here we have a secure site, water, electricity, toilets, showers and good access to the M62 and beyond. There have been several management changes over the years. The first manager, Richard Exley, through his ambition to run a posh, south coast marina, devoted his efforts towards yachties and looked down on cruiser owners. He achieved his ambition. His successor, Howard, was a generous gentleman, much more even-handed than his predecessor. Yard foreman, Bob Bass served the early managers and could be uncooperative at times but was generally helpful to us when Mad Max was not around.

The marina thrived and was host to Power Boat Races, Round the World Yachts, Sea Shanties and Jazz Festivals. When the Council became bored with the Marina, they leased it to British Waterways, an organisation steeped in tradition. Hull represented a change of culture for British Waterways whose expertise lay inland with canals. But gradually the management has adapted and become more customer orientated. The current management, Barry, Carolyn and the yard operatives are helpful and supportive.

Sharing the site with us for many years is the friendly, family run Kildale Marine; chandlers, riggers, dog lovers, sympathetic listeners and all round good folk. The owners, Richard and Sue always have time for a friendly word. C-Tec Marine Services, another family outfit, also work in and around the marina and are often a source of work for us.

In and around the Humber Estuary there are a number of marinas and boatyards. Grimsby, another recycled commercial dock is home to the thriving Humber Cruising Association with a hoist and a bar, both operated by friendly, helpful staff. Situated near the southern end of the Humber Bridge at the mouth of a tributary river, the Ancholme, is South Ferriby Marina, the scene of dramatic, perhaps even scary crane operations, first by Rodney Clapson, now by Paddy Ferguson.

Further up the Ancholme, Glanford Boat Club has a strong, vibrant membership. We have many good friends and customers there, some using us every year to relocate their boat for a season or a holiday. Ross Seargent was a regular customer who often put his wife in the cab to ride 'shotgun' with us. She always came equipped with plenty of 'snap' and she introduced us to Soreen, a delicious malt loaf. This, together with our cheese and Marmite sarnies became the premium 'pack up' and may well have included two of our required 'Five a Day'.

Budgie, Mick Nolan and others are regular Brigg customers. The 'Crane Days' at Brigg are a sight to behold. Dozens of boats are lifted in a morning of frenzied, disciplined precision activity. If ever there were to be 'Synchronised Craning' as an Olympics event, the team at Brigg would surely win Gold.

However, it has been suggested that the committee, and committees in many other boat clubs, may be affiliated to the Mafia but nevertheless the club is extremely well run!

At the head of the Humber lies Goole, a port and town built at the start of the Aire and Calder Navigation, a waterway connecting with the Yorkshire Coalfield. Here, we visit Viking Marine, which has a hoist and nearby lie The Boathouse and Heck Basin, all generating boat movements. Our Hiab equipped colleague, Steve Tennant, prowls these waterways with his cruiser and the boatyards with his crane.

Goole is also where the Yorkshire Ouse and the River Trent meet to become the Humber. Our main destination on the Ouse, is Naburn, just south of York, where new owners have modernised the facilities over the last few years. The previous owners Mr and Mrs. Poole were reluctant to invest. When coerced into providing showers the first installation required a fifty pence piece. There is nothing unusual in that, except it was an old fifty pence that was needed, resulting in a visit to the chandlery for a suitable coin! Naburn has been a good source of work for many years, with craft arriving from or dispersing to the upper parts of the river. Raymond Howe organises the lifting facilities and has long been the source of good advice about boats and boat owners.

The River Trent has been a commercial waterway for centuries providing navigation into the heart of England. It has numerous marinas and boatyards plus canals, 'cuts' and dykes connecting with many distant areas. Newark on Trent is almost our second home as Newark Marina has been the source of much work over the years and is often used as a safe haven. James Wilkinson and his team have been generous to us providing safe parking and hoisting facilities. 'Q' often ends up at Newark on a Tuesday night to play Bingo at a local pub, even when he's supposed to be somewhere else. Nearby Farndon Marina was set up by Mark Ainsworth, who was a far-sighted pioneer of recreational boating facilities, as well as boat transport. Mark was a barge skipper, working on the Trent and saw the potential in the old gravel pits. Sadly, Mark is no longer with us but his son Paul now runs this fine marina. We are regular visitors there also and are well treated.

The Fossdyke is a cut running eastwards from the Trent to Lincoln and beyond, which permits access to Burton Waters Marina, a spectacular re-use of gravel workings. The complex comprises housing, shops, sports centre, pub, moorings, hoist, chandlery and all marina facilities set in a landscaped area designed to protect and enhance wildlife. Peter King and his boat broking team sell many boats from there and pass a lot of jobs in our direction.

A cut running westward from the Trent, the South Yorkshire Navigation passes through Thorne. Here, Stanilands Marina was for a while a big source of work. Bob Hammerton and Geoff Pannal, boating friends, bought this marina and transformed it from a maritime backwater into a thriving club and busy yard. We still work with Martin and Helen the current owners.

The Norfolk Broads is the heartland of hire boating and we are in and out of Brundall, almost like a bus service. With very few exceptions, Broads people are friendly and helpful. Broom Boats encompass the full range of marine activities. They build quality motor cruisers, have a hire fleet, a hoist and showers.

Brundall Bay Marina has good parking, a hoist and showers but Neil often finds it too far to walk from there to the Yare, the only pub in the village.

Norfolk Yacht Agency has its main office there and its own service centre for the preparation and maintenance of boats. Despite 'Q' having the reputation as the 'rain-bringer' and Paul's failure to honour his pledge to valet the staff vehicles, we enjoy a great working relationship with James Frazer and his gang at Brundall, and also at Horning. Dafney had the honour of starring in their promotion film.

We have been privileged to work with Bell Boats for probably longer than any other Broadlands business, often moving their own Aquabell workboats or craft for private customers. They are another friendly Brundall business.

The tight squeeze into Burgh Castle is worth it to work with Goodchild Marine Services, a fine enterprise run by Alan and Sue Goodchild and their ever-cheerful staff.

Anglia Yacht Brokers at St. Olaves marina also provide our drivers with parking, showers and efficient loading facilities.

There are several other marinas and boatyards we visit on the Broads and we give priority to those where it is 'Standing Orders' to offer the driver a cup of tea.

Fenland sites around Huntingdon and Bedford have several excellent marinas. Les, Elaine and Graham run Westview Marina at Earith and always show hospitality to our drivers. Nearby, Buckden Marina and Hartford Marina are equally welcoming.

The Thames is a very popular boating river and we regularly deliver upstream from London. Destinations in the big city itself are now more or less denied us due to the restrictions of the Low Emission Zone. Any movement within the LEZ incurs a charge of £200 per day, whilst movements of wide loads within the entire Metropolitan Police area are subject to rush hour curfews.

Penton Hook and Shepperton Marinas are close to the M25, just outside the LEZ and the Nightime Lorry Ban. These bans and restrictions don't help the job, that's for sure!

Upstream there lies Racecourse Marina, Windsor with good parking apart from Mondays in the summer when horse racing takes place. Near the gate is a Harvester pub, boil in the bag stuff in the main, but handy. Bray is famous for its cuisine, way beyond the pocket of our drivers and the nearest pub is miles away. Espar Marine operate a crane and hoist at Harleyford Marina, where the showers are excellent and sometimes the floating restaurant is open. Otherwise a long walk into Marlow is required. Still further upstream, there are two marinas at Reading, both with limited facilities for drivers. The highest loading point on the Thames with a permanent crane is Eynsham with a difficult reverse on the blind side!

Further west on the rivers Severn and Avon boating is a major activity. Our deliveries take us to Bristol, Gloucester, Tewkesbury, Upton and Stourport, each a delightful resort.

There was one inland boat centre that provided us with a lot of boats but had no water! Nationwide Boat Sales, near Chesterfield claimed to sell more boats than any other place in Europe. Indeed it had a reputation for a quick turnaround at modest cost and we know of many people who started boating with a 'Nationwide' deal. Long gone and replaced by housing, a business missed by bargain-seeking boaters.

Britain's maritime expansion created harbours and docks for commercial and military use. As the nation has declined industrially and defence needs have changed the facilities have fallen into disuse. The redundant docks have in many cases been revitalised as marinas, breathing new life into old industrial areas.

The Victorians developed the concept of seaside holidays, so resorts sprang up around the coast to receive the hordes from the industrial centres. Our visits to these centres of recreational activity are obviously stressful and tiring.

Bridlington is a near neighbour with clean sandy beaches and a small harbour. The hoist is reached via a tight entrance but there are pubs, chippies and cafes nearby.

Dracula, Goths, Heartbeat and Captain Cook all helped to make Whitby famous. Whaling was once a major industry, but now wailing of another kind emanates from the pubs during the Sea Shanty and Folk Music weeks. Summer or winter it's always good to be there; a town of great character with excellent fish and chips, pubs with good beer, pubs with good music and friendly people with a sense of humour. Oh, and the good people at Coates Marine where we load or unload.

Hartlepool Marina is another good example of the revival of an old dock. Modern developments include restaurants of international cuisine, cafes and shops. Nearby, the Small Crafts Club or 'Smallies' has cheap beer, bingo and karaoke nights. In the boatyard Gary and Colin have given us great service over many years and the marina is a credit to Alan and his team. As they say themselves, "Hartlepool, a marina and much more".

The landscape around the River Tyne has changed dramatically in recent years, being transformed from a centre of heavy industry to an area of vibrant modern culture. Our drivers obviously belong in such an environment. Near the mouth of the Tyne, at North Shields lies the Royal Quays Marina. If there was a training manual for marina operators, this would be the model upon which it would be based. Matt Simms, Brian Wilkes and staff are customer focused and friendly. They have provided us with flexibility, adaptability and old fashioned courtesy from the day the marina opened. The floating pub, The Earl of Zetland usually has good beer and when the Zetland is not serving food it is but a short walk to the Premier Inn.

Scotland, the boat transport fiefdom of John Shepherd, is blessed with dozens of little harbours, originally perhaps the home to fishing boats, now occupied by recreational boaters. Some have become fully-fledged marinas, others just offer basic requirements; water and wind.

The Clyde is a well-established boating area with marinas such as Troon, Ardrossan, Largs and Inverkip. Apart from the beautiful scenery, the facilities for customers and hauliers are excellent. Largs was the site of the last Viking battle and boat burning is an annual ritual to celebrate this event. The crowd once claimed that I was carrying the boat chosen for the ritual and demanded the right to burn it. Eventually, they accepted that fibreglass wouldn't ignite very easily so I was allowed to leave. The Clydeside marinas are reasonably accessible by road but the marinas in North West Scotland around Oban are more difficult to reach. These could be the 'Mountains, Lochs and Glens' tours that less fortunate people have to pay for. Apart from the long distances involved, several low bridges cross the poor roads. Other hazards include logging vehicles, caravaners, ('Q' is one you know), wild deer and sometimes wild kilted Scotsmen.

Craobhaven is a custom built traditional village with well-serviced marina attached. Ardfern was the site of Q's infamous weekend away, which led to his exclusion from Scottish jobs.

Dunstaffnage, to the north of Oban boasts the second bravest hoist operator in Scotland, defying gale force winds to unload Dobbin. The first bravest is Duncan Pockett, the manager at Lossiemouth Marina who unloaded Dafney during an incredible storm, dismissing the gale as a summer breeze.

Inverness, at the northern end of the Caledonian Canal, boasts two marinas, Caley Marine at the top of the locks and Longmans Harbour at sea level. These would be 'Highland Heritage' tours for anyone else.

Cumbria, mainly served by Andy Brown, the local boat haulier, has the boating centres of 'The Lakes' plus the revived industrial ports of Whitehaven and Maryport, both with thriving marinas.

Fleetwood Marina in Lancashire has shared the Fish Dock for many years but recent investment has enhanced the facilities for boaters and even hauliers.

We often work with Blue Point Marine who operate the hoist at Liverpool Marina.

The coast of Wales resembles Scotland in some respects with many small harbours developing leisure activities. Conwy, Deganwy, Bangor, Holyhead and Pwllheli are frequent destinations in the north, all now with well-developed marinas. For what it's worth, Tommy, the crane man from Conwy once met 'Q' on top of the Empire State Building.

Then there is the long swaithe of Cardigan Bay where access is difficult and only rarely visited. The Milford Haven, Swansea and Cardiff areas are more accessible and the people seem less inclined to use the Welsh language than their compatriots in the North and the roads are better too.

The West Country has numerous attractions, many of them involving water. Fishing, sailing and cruising will bring us into the region. Portishead, Watchet and Padstow serve the north coast. Falmouth, Torquay, Darthaven and Plymouth are our main destinations in the south. Not content with 'working' in the area, Paul, Sue and Alex take their holidays around Dartmouth. And why not? Boarding one of the cross-river ferries transports one back in time to a more friendly era.

The Clovelly Arms near Plymouth Yacht Haven serves great food and beer, has a superb vintage jukebox and delightful staff. Obviously, this in no way influences our preference of this destination.

The coast from Devon to Kent has more marinas than any other area so naturally it generates a lot of our work. Portland has excellent facilities due to Olympic investment and road access has even been improved. Until recently, an escorted diversion took us across an army training range and it was not unusual to find a Challenger Tank hiding in the hedge. Poole Harbour has several marinas and boatyards. 'Q' will probably retire to this area, maybe to Sandbanks.

The Solent boasts yards and marinas for every type of boat from sailing dinghies to super-yachts. Shamrock Quay, Moodys, RK Marine, Gosport Boatyard and Port Solent are our preferred sites.

Sussex is Terry Ollerton country but occasionally when his back is turned or he is abroad we can get trips to Chichester, Brighton, Newhaven and lots of little boatyards in the county.

Kent is a regular destination either to rescue sailors who have bottled out from sailing into the North Sea or to visit the many boatyards around the historic River Medway, in particular our good friends at Gillingham Marina.

Essex, with its myriad of creeks and muddy estuaries is a busy boat owning area being so close to London. Suffolk has important marinas around Ipswich making the A14 a regularly used road for us. Seeing the container lorries grinding remorselessly along this road serves to give a happy reminder of our good fortune. We are heading for civilisation, not Felixstowe docks.

It hardly seems right but we get paid for this too. We are extremely lucky.

CHAPTER EIGHTEEN

Any Way The Wind Blows

After seventeen chapters looking back, I'd like to conclude with a view of the present and some hopes for the future.

I belong to the most privileged generation ever. Born after the war but soon enough to enjoy the Fifties and Sixties when, for the most part anyway, things just got better. Free school milk, free education, free love (really?) and burgeoning opportunity, created a society with standards of living that previous generations never even dreamt of. Full employment, fashion, music and increased leisure time led the charge from austerity to affluence. This may have been maintained by false optimism and bad governance but the party rolled on until after the millennium. It makes a poor pun, but riding the crest of the wave had to stop when the wave broke, or put another way, when the bubble burst, in 2008.

Being part of this 'overblown' economy as it could be described did not make our fortunes as employees or management but gave us a working environment that our contemporaries in general haulage would envy. Our flight from supermarket abuse is a theme mentioned more than once. However, my flippant remarks that boat transport 'is just not work', must be taken with a pinch of salt. Indeed, loading is both physically and mentally draining and the safe carriage of not just valuable goods, but prized personal possessions, adds a heavy burden of responsibility onto the drivers.

Time takes its toll and bodies wear out. I am now

consigned mainly to the office and trips out with Paul are subject to stringent conditions, and my being 'cable-tied' to the seat for personal and/or public safety. Beating anorexia but succumbing to senility, I must hand over the reins to the next generation. Hopefully, Neil will continue to work to the good of the business as he has since 1987 and take himself to a well-earned retirement when he is ready. Paul has already introduced more stringent maintenance and compliance procedures and has established a reputation for care and diligence. Sue has taken over most of the bookkeeping and has computerised our accounts. Some important costs have been identified and pared. The efficiency of the business has therefore increased and there are definite grounds for optimism.

There is still a reasonable amount of work about but conditions are the hardest and harshest that they have ever been. Every job has to be fought for and competition is fiercer than ever. Customers are more demanding and some devious behaviour has crept in. Bad debt is on the increase.

The Internet has been a mixed blessing. Communication is faster for sure but e-mails take the personal involvement out of negotiations. Websites offering transport via a bidding process only go one way, downwards. This would seem to be advantageous to the customer but it may well leave them with a spurious operator and definitely under-insured.

Banking attitudes leave me bewildered. After our struggles in the 80s and early 90s, we have remained solvent since before the turn of the century, recording a small profit each year. This year, in trying to raise finance for a trailer replacement, our good record counted for nothing. Loan offers were subject to stringent conditions, interest rates way above base, and would have just about covered the cost of the wheels. We found a way eventually from our own resources but what hope is there for anyone struggling or trying to get a start?

Thankfully, it is not all doom and gloom. We continue to receive repeat business from long standing customers, both commercial and private. Perhaps we should issue a 'Loyalty Card'.

There are still fish left in the sea and there will always be someone prepared to catch them. People will still relax by messing about on boats and intrepid sailors will relish the challenge, 'whichever way the wind blows'. Hopefully though, there will always be customers prepared to put their *keels* on our *wheels*.